To Pat

D0747178

TWO BUTTS ON A BIKE

Enjoy the Ride

Rick & Christie
Gorsline

TWO BUTTS
ON A BIKE

4 MONTHS, 18 COUNTRIES, 12,074 MILES

PORTLAND•OREGON
INKWATERPRESS.COM

RICK AND CHRISTIE GORSLINE

*Scan this QR Code
to learn more about
this title*

Cover and interior design by Emily Dueker
Motorcycle © Elyasaf. Dreamstime.com

Publisher: Inkwater Press

Paperback
ISBN-13 978-1-59299-859-3 | ISBN-10 1-59299-859-3

Hardcover
ISBN-13 978-1-59299-860-9 | ISBN-10 1-59299-860-7

Kindle
ISBN-13 978-1-59299-861-6 | ISBN-10 1-59299-861-5

Printed in the U.S.A.
All paper is acid free and meets all ANSI standards for archival quality paper.

1 3 5 7 9 10 8 6 4 2

NOTES FROM THE AUTHORS

Rick: A good thing about motorcycle travel is that when you get off you're wearing the right shoes to hike. And, in a pinch, cycle boots make adequate, if embarrassing, golf shoes.

Christie: Part of the magic for me was that our plan defied society's expectations. I'd waited to have babies until after marriage and obligingly joined the Junior League. But somewhere deep inside, a rebel must have been lurking and she waited until middle age to act out. A motorcycle ride across Europe was the perfect venue. The problem was that once she emerged there was no putting her back.

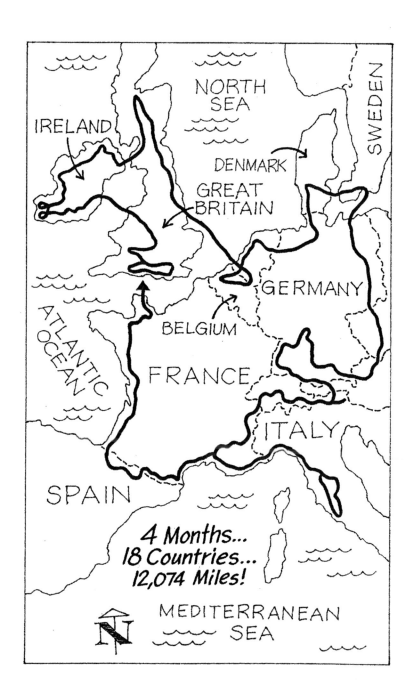

IRELAND

NORTH SEA

SWEDEN

DENMARK

GREAT BRITAIN

ATLANTIC OCEAN

BELGIUM

GERMANY

FRANCE

ITALY

SPAIN

4 Months...
18 Countries...
12,074 Miles!

N

MEDITERRANEAN SEA

CONTENTS

DEDICATION

To Christie:
"You're an awesome girl and the trip was a blast." - Rick

To Rick:
"Thank you for helping me find my true North." – Christie

Our thanks to –

Joanna Rose who helped so much with story arc and pacing. Her encouragement kept the story flowing.

Lee Zinsli, who scanned our photos and got them ready for the publisher.

Paul A. Combs, who came to the rescue with hand-drawn maps when we learned that our maps were copyrighted and couldn't be used in the book.

We owe a huge debt of gratitude to Joanna, Lee and Paul but also to Inkwater Press who believed in the project.

And to you – our readers. Without you there would be no reason to find the words to describe our experiences. We hope you, too, enjoy the ride.

This book is the second Gorsline adventure travel book; it follows *Empty Nest to Life Vest: Plotting a New Course*, published in 2010.

Reader note: The text is in two fonts. One is the voice of Rick and the other is Christie. Reading in an e-version might override the print format. We apologize for any confusion.

"Don't worry 'bout what you don't know. Life's a dance you learn as you go."

– JOHN MICHAEL MONTGOMERY

CHAPTER 1

ON YOUR MARK, GET SET...

IT WAS A crisp fall day and Rick's 56th birthday. I rubbed my thumb back and forth on the soft leather of my new jacket. I loved the smell and the Harley logo made me feel adventuresome.

Lots of decisions in our marriage had been mine but what kind of motorcycle to buy for a four-month ride across Europe was not. I rocked from one foot to the other, excited by the prospect of the trip but otherwise bored by hours of guy-speak and bantering.

We test-drove bike after bike and Rick kept asking me how it felt. "Not as good as our old Kawasaki," I told him. But it didn't matter. I'd get used to whatever he chose.

"As long as it's a bright color so we'll be visible," I said.

WE NEEDED A motorcycle that could handle both of us and a mountain of gear. The obvious choice was to buy in Europe and I looked into it. Insurance would cost less and we'd save shipping fees. But riding two-up meant there were two decision makers and Christie had made it clear that she wanted a trial run. Her efficient side balked at the idea of spending "Europe time" shopping for a bike.

She wanted to see how the gear fit in the saddle bags and to take a few rides before we got to Europe. And she's my wife, so her opinion mattered.

WHEN THE SUN made its curtain call, the moon gave a silver-edge to the clouds, and Rick's birthday present, a brand new red BMW R1100GS, glowed in the waning light. She had a long red front fender so I christened her "Woody" for Woody Woodpecker. She needed bigger saddle bags and a taller windshield. But we had time and Rick was good at those kinds of details.

WE NEEDED CAMPING gear and a tank bag. Lightweight clothing we could layer. I tried to estimate the weight of two riders, a tent, two sleeping bags, lantern, camp stove, books, guide books, camera, and shower gear. The bike could only carry 100 pounds in addition to the two of us.

We needed a bike cover that was small enough to store when it wasn't in use and a way to secure the helmets and leathers. It was when Christie started talking about books and extra shoes that I knew we were in trouble. I made a note to take a tire pressure gauge. With all that weight I'd be checking it often.

SIX MONTHS AFTER we bought Woody, Rick had installed a taller windshield and we'd agreed on a saddle bag design. The custom Jesse bags were metal with a rectangular upright profile and hinged lids that flipped open to make a flat, makeshift table. I squinted into one of the little boxes. Mine was the one on the right. It was barely big enough for six medium boxes of cereal if you crushed the corners. It would hold everything I would take on a four-month tour. Anguishing over what I wouldn't be able to take, I plotted space for an extra pair of shoes.

I ORDERED BRACKETS welded to the top of the Jesse bags so we could bungee the sleeping mats in waterproof bags on top. We bought used camping gear and I got an international driver's license at the AAA office. We'd heard that if your license was taken by the police, having two was good insurance.

We marched forward and the "to do" list evolved day to day. One thing was certain: it wasn't like planning a two-week vacation. We plotted our route only in a general sense, knowing that fate would dictate the itinerary.

APRIL 13 I shoved the Thermarests® into their red vinyl waterproof bags and bungeed them to the tops of the saddle bags. The rolled-up tent was in its own black waterproof bag and rode on top of the rear bag. A BMW is a stately machine but with our gear strapped on, it looked like a top-heavy pack mule.

Log entry, *"Tucson, Arizona, shake down. Tire pressure good but the rear shock needs air. First stop, gas station."*

I DON'T KNOW why I hadn't thought of it as we accumulated the gear but it came to me in a rush when the bike was loaded and I was supposed to hop on.

"Honey, we've got a little problem back here," I said in what might have been a whine. I'm only 5'2" and the loaded bike hit me at chest height. My high-kicking dance team days were thirty-five years and twenty pounds in the past. I had no idea how to mount the beast.

"Use your high school, Rockette leg lift," Rick chuckled.

"Yeah, right," I grumbled. "This'll take a helicopter."

"Put your foot on the peg and go slowly," he instructed without looking back. Balancing the heavy bike took concentration. The BMW GS model is tall and it's ideal if your height is in your legs, which his isn't. With his heels off the ground, he held the bike upright, waiting for me to get on.

I inhaled deeply and held my breath. With my left hand on Rick's shoulder and my left foot on the peg, I swung my right leg as high as a short gal could muster and gently lowered myself into the cocoon behind him. And exhaled.

"All set?" Rick asked, patting my knee and firing up the motor.

"Yeah, I think so," I murmured. I leaned back against the rear bag and realized that the waterproof duffle made a nice back rest. And the bags that held the bedrolls were perfect armrests. I giggled but decided to keep the extent of my comfort to myself.

RIDING TWO-UP WITH full gear, the bike was top-heavy. At lunch I told Christie that if she moved with me in the turns the bike might feel less like a camel ride. We'd had very little riding experience so I drew a picture on a paper napkin. She's a bright girl and quickly

grasped the concept of swaying in the turns instead of sitting bolt upright like a counterweight.

It rained buckets. We rode northwest through Wickenburg and stopped in Sedona. The second-hand tent leaked. Our sleeping bags turned to sponges. God might have been warning us but we didn't pay attention.

In the morning, we spread the soggy camp gear on a picnic table and anchored it with rocks. We rode into town for breakfast, past enormous red cliffs streaked with horizontal lines of yellow and grey. I tried to sway with Rick in the turns but got distracted by the view. I tipped my head back to take in the enormity and flipping my helmet's face mask open, I drank in the craggy hilltops, imagining them into the shapes of Scottish castles.

A realtor's "Open House" sign caught Christie's attention. She leaned forward and hollered, "Let's go look at that house." It felt good to get off the bike and stretch my legs but I wasn't sure we needed to be looking at real estate.

We hadn't owned a home since our daughters left for college seven years earlier. We'd lived on a sailboat for six years, four of them off the west coast of Mexico. The vagrant life was pretty ingrained.

With leather jackets and helmets slung over our arms we walked into the Santa Fe–style house. Thick adobe walls, a kiva fireplace in the living room, and Saltillo tile floors were features I'd always liked. Christie was ahead of me, upstairs in the master bedroom. I knew we were in trouble when she called down the stairs, "The view up here is fabulous, honey, come take a look." I should have known better. She was right. The red cliffs looked close enough to touch. We made an offer that afternoon.

I was giddy at the prospect of having a home. I'd loved our boating years and the Airstream trailer was fine but the suburbanite in me was calling. I was ready for furniture, bookcases, and a real refrigerator.

Seated on a pew at Sedona's Chapel of the Holy Cross, I turned to face Rick.

"Motorcycle riding is dangerous business," he said, taking both of my hands in his. I looked down at our interlocking fingers. Rick bowed his head and began, "God, please watch out for us and protect us on this journey."

"And give Rick careful driving skills," I said. I looked up at him, "And give me silence in times of angst."

He smiled, kissed my eyebrow and squeezed my fingers. "And patience to both of us."

We stood to go. "We'll need lots of that. We're talking 24/7, just inches apart."

"That part'll be easy after six years on the boat," he said and I laughed, shading my eyes from the bright sun. "The hardest part right now for me is that if we come home with missing limbs, or worse, we have only ourselves to blame."

In response to Christie's misgivings, I crooned a little Jimmy Buffett. *"I'd rather die while I'm living than live while I'm dead."* She wasn't amused and kicked me in the shin.

Secretly, I didn't think Jimmy wanted to pay the price either. But I wanted to see Europe and a motorcycle would add to the fun and keep costs down. "Could-a-should-a" was about the worst epitaph I could imagine.

We left Sedona before the realtor could tell us if our offer had been accepted. I felt like we'd dodged a bullet.

We rode to Payson and stayed in a motel for its dry bed, shower, and TV. The next morning, a SWAT team locked down the parking lot while they arrested our neighbors. Being confined gave us time to talk.

"Christie, I'd like a house, too, but it seems kind of crazy to take such a big step when we're leaving the country for four months."

"I know. Logically," she sighed. "But I'd be comforted to know what life I'm returning to."

I lifted the blinds and saw that the officers had holstered their guns. I put my arm around Christie and kissed the top of her head. "You always want answers when we don't even know the questions. As to where we'll want to live when we get back next fall? Who knows? With AJ on the East Coast and Lisa on the West anything's possible."

Back in Tucson, I wrote in my Log. "Put 1,103 miles on Woody. I'm more confident. We don't have an itinerary, just some maps and notes from guide books. We'll take advice from those we meet and hope for the best. Our only reservation is a return plane ticket." God help us.

"Your work is to discover your world and then with all your heart give yourself to it."

– BUDDHA

CHAPTER 2

GO!

WE SPED NORTH on I-5 toward Canada, buffeted by a head-wind of possibilities. Rain came in long vertical slaps so I huddled low. Under a steel wool sky, Rick ducked behind the windshield but the downpour blurred his view and water swooshed under our wheels. It was an absurd way to start a long trip. Rivers ran into my boots. I wiggled my toes to ward off a creeping numbing and grimaced at the feel of squishy socks.

We were flying out of Vancouver B.C. to London's Gatwick airport. The motorcycle would ride as cargo on the same plane.

AT THE HOTEL, we off-loaded 95 pounds, 43 kilos, of gear. A tent, sleeping bags, and foam mats with stays that turned them into ground level chairs. Stainless coffee cups that would do triple duty as wine glasses and soup mugs. A camp stove, lantern and a couple of forks, bowls, and cloth napkins completed the household supplies. Shirts, shorts, and long pants were rolled in zip-lock bags. All our toiletries, medicines and a small piece of chamois toweling were tightly packed in waterproof bags. For the flight, it all would go as checked luggage in old army duffle bags.

PACKING HAD BEEN an adventure.

"You've only got one saddlebag," Rick had said, eyeing the pile of clothes I was certain I needed but wistfully left behind.

The bike had to be checked-in 24 hours before take-off so we put the helmets back on our wet heads and rode to the cargo office. I was relieved when we were greeted with a big smile like he was expecting us.

A SMALL TEAM examined our paperwork and checked that the fuel tank was less than half-full, and I disconnected the battery.

The Canadian cargo fellow went inside the container. He guided the handlebars while I pushed. He expertly secured the tie-down straps and I looked on in admiration. This wasn't his first rodeo but it certainly was mine. When he climbed out, I said,

"Thank you so much," offering my hand. We shook and I had a good feeling that Woody would arrive standing upright.

We headed back to the hotel. I held my soggy gloves in one hand and Christie's hand in the other. Our helmets hung over our arms. Helmets are mandatory in Europe and I'd read a story about a guy who got his stolen when he was miles from anywhere to buy a replacement. Using a pilfered hotel towel and duct tape he fabricated one and rode into the next town. From a distance it would have looked like a rather odd-shaped white helmet. I didn't want to do that so Christie had our names airbrushed on ours. Her logic was that if they were stolen, the graphics might make recovery possible.

RAIN RAN DOWN the sleeve of my jacket and into my helmet but my mind was on the future. I was eager to explore the rocky coast of Ireland and to hike in Switzerland. We would ride the mountain passes of the Alps and maybe the Dolomites. Rick planned to buy stickers along the way and to decorate the saddle bags with them. We would stay in small inns on occasion but mostly in campgrounds. We weren't experienced Europe travelers but we hoped to be when we returned.

"If not now, when?"

– CHRISTIE'S GRANDMOTHER,
ELSIE THELMA WELTER, 1901–1982

CHAPTER 3

WEEK ONE

JUNE 1 Boarding the plane, a cranky fellow traveler didn't want our stuff in his overhead space. Sorry I couldn't smack him with my helmet.

BY THE TIME the plane was airborne, a broken armrest took precedence over thoughts of where we'd live when we returned. I pulled a spiral journal from my bag. I wrote, *"June 1,"* and put the pen down. On September 28 we would fly the return route and these pages would be full. Miles of roads would have been traveled. Adventures and mishaps. Good wine and bad food. Wrong turns and rainbows. But now the pages were blank.

OUR PLAN WHEN the girls had gone to college was to abandon suburbia and to sail around the world. For six years, *Nanook,* our 37-foot sailboat, was home. An image of waving palm trees and white sand beaches might appear here but the reality was storms, a balky engine, and our own lack of sailing experience. We never left the west coast of Mexico, so, I

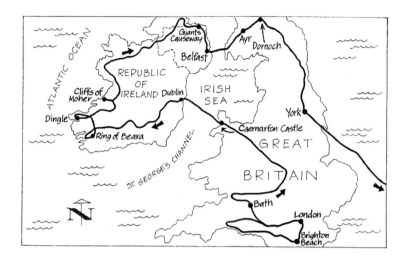

reasoned, the world was still waiting for us. Hence the birth of Plan B, a motorcycle lap around Europe.

IN LONDON, WE followed the signs to baggage claim, retrieved our checked luggage, and shuffled through customs. Christie headed for a bank of phones while I held our place in the taxi queue.

"GAINSBOROUGH GUEST HOUSE" was a random choice and luck was with us. They had a room, and yes, they'd be there "quite rightly." We dragged the duffle bags out of the taxi queue and moved 100 yards down the sidewalk to wait.

I fell gratefully onto the soft mattress but sleep was elusive. In a state of dazed exhaustion I accepted jet lag as an ugly aspect of travel and headed to town.

LIKE A HANGOVER, jet lag went away in its own time.

JUNE 2   A platter of scrambled eggs, grilled tomatoes, sausage, bacon, and beans took the edge off my travel fatigue. Much later in the trip, gnawing on hard rolls and trying to get used to German bologna and cold cheeses, we would remember British breakfasts with nostalgia. But that first morning, we took a hot breakfast for granted.

We rode back to the airport in the inn's van and got out at the cargo office. I completed more paperwork, Rick paid the duty bill, and we strode the few hundred yards to the British customs depot. And waited. After what seemed like an eternity, Woody's metal box rolled out.

TAKING HER OUT wasn't as smooth as the departure had been. The Brit was uninterested in helping. At 600 pounds, it was going to be a monster to unstrap on my own. While I was scratching my head about how to handle the task with just Christie's help, a nice fellow stepped up. I was grateful and gave him a hearty handshake and "thank you." It was way too early to drop the bike.

WHILE RICK'S ATTENTION was on connecting the battery and setting the clock, I watched a hearse slowly back toward the container. A uniformed driver got out and wheeled a shiny black casket with ornate brass handles into Woody's crate. I shivered and turned away.

WE HEADED TO Brighton Beach for our British shake down. Driving on the left side was pretty easy when I followed the car in front of me. It was only when the car exited where I hadn't meant to that it got complicated.

At the first petrol stop I remembered that an Imperial gallon is a quart more than our gallon. Lots of change to get used to.

DWARF CARS DARTED like jackrabbits, hopping in and out of lanes like children playing dodge ball. Rick handled it calmly but I heard him muttering, "Left, left, left." It was going to take practice. Adding to the confusion was that intersections had roundabouts, not stop lights. They were efficient once you got used to them except when we found ourselves spit-out by accident and had to find our way back. From my rear perch, I had a great view over Rick's shoulders and around his helmet. Despite jet lag and apprehension, my cheeks ached from the foolish grin I wore.

A HEALTH RESORT during the 18th century, Brighton became a destination for day trippers from London after the arrival of the railway in 1841. The sun was out but there was a distinct chill in the stiff breeze. We rented fabric sling chairs and bought fish and chips in brown paper. A good start.

WE MUNCHED OUR greasy lunch and watched a parade of Brits strolling the rocky beach. The men wore jackets that looked too small and ladies, mid-calf dark skirts. The young were heavily pierced and tattooed, sporting rainbow-colored hair. Everything seemed extreme but maybe I was observing more intently than I did at home.

Leaving the coast, we pulled into a rest stop filled with motorcycles. Ducatis, Suzukis, a BMW much like ours, and Hondas. Not a Harley in sight. They seemed to be out for a casual ride but were dressed like racers with flames on their helmets. These were serious bikers. They admired ours, completely amazed that we were from the United States. A tall, lean Englishman, decked out in head-to-toe red and black leathers, suggested we visit a Roman villa nearby. I vowed to find it.

Just up the road, we stopped in quaint Chichester. I ran a cable through our helmets and jacket sleeves, tethering them to the bike. Christie helped me snap the thin nylon cover over the windshield and seat. She called it a hair net. It wasn't the best security system but it was easy to store and I hoped it was adequate.

A flower show had taken over the village. Pots of apricot lilies, roses the size of peonies, stalks of lavender, and mountains of sweet peas crowded tables up and down the cobbled lane. I loved the sweet aroma and the sight of ladies with open-sided baskets over their arms. They wore flowered dresses, flowered scarves, and sweaters that buttoned up the front. I was glad I wasn't carrying a helmet.

Crossing a bridge, we paused just to watch the river flow beneath. Walking slowly on, we passed the wheel of an old mill and a yellowed stone building that now housed a craft shop. Next door was a gallery and the red-striped awning of a café caught my eye. We settled at a sidewalk table, ordered limeades and pastries. Folks surged past, looking focused. By contrast, I had no place to be or people expecting anything from me. I smiled at the thought. We had no commitments except to each other.

WE DETOURED AT Bignor to see the villa recommended by the guy on the Ducati. It was the enormous remains of a Roman home and farm. World-class mosaic floors indoors and the out-buildings had thatched roofs and carved hedges that seemed to go on for miles.

Back at the Gainsborough inn, we walked into Horsley, through a 600-year-old cemetery, stopping at a 500-year-old pub. The restaurant seemed to specialize in something served in a glazed brown pot because nearly every table had one. We ordered the brown pot and enjoyed a fine steak and kidney pie.

JUNE 3 After another hearty British breakfast, I packed up while Christie took our folded duffle bags to the manager for storage. With luck, we'd be back for them in four months.

I put the first sticker on the bike, a small red and white Canadian maple leaf I'd bought at the Vancouver airport. Riding toward Bath, England, in light rain, I smiled. "Wow, what a feeling. 118 days to go."

I kept our speed at about 65 mph but cars passed on the right as if we were slow. The roundabouts were beginning to be a habit by the time we got to Salisbury.

WALKING THROUGH SALISBURY, I looked up to marvel at the tallest spire in England and tripped on the cobblestones but Rick caught me. Salisbury cathedral took thirty years to build in the early 1200s. Inside, we examined the original Magna Carta and the world's oldest working clock. Wet surfaces glistened; we strolled and ate meat pies on the square.

JUST A SHORT hop to Stonehenge. One glance told me that it was one of those "Eiffel Tower-Mt. Rushmore" places. That's what Christie called sights that looked exactly like the postcard, making you wonder why you'd bothered. The stone pillars stood on end in a circular arrangement and are believed to have been erected around 2,500 B.C. We could see them through the fence.

We were waiting to buy tickets when, as the Brits would say, "A lorry load of foreigners descended." It was a swarm of Japanese tourists. They surged into the ticket queue ahead of us. After about ten minutes we still hadn't gotten to the pay station. "This is annoying," I said to Christie.

"There's another version I read about with no admission charge," she whispered. "It's just up the road." That's all it took. We were gone.

Avebury is larger than Stonehenge, with no tickets to buy and no crowds. The stone circle is older, too and it's near a village with a picture book manor. That checked a lot of boxes in my book.

IT WAS JUST us, a flock of angora goats and the rocks. Being utterly alone gave the place the drama that was missing at Stonehenge. The monoliths were already ancient history when the Romans ruled England. I wanted to stay but all of Europe stretched in front of us so we got back on the bike.

Four miles from Bath we settled on our first campground at a daily fee of $12 for Woody and two people. It had a narrow stream running through and was said to be the site of Roman washing pools.

I asked for a camp space but instead of assigning one, the woman waved a gnarled hand in the direction of the field, saying "Go on now, you young uns. Plop you' tent 'n make youself a' home. Tea'll be ready qwat rightly."

Do we pay now, I wondered? Is there an assigned space? The answer was apparently "no" to both. With no amenities like tables or chairs, camping didn't involve delineated spaces. We rode across the field and parked at the foot of a small hill.

The grass covered my boots and smelled like clover. Rick surveyed the site, deciding where it was the flattest and which way the tent should face. I pulled the bungees off the red waterproof bags that were my armrests and together we tugged the Thermarest® mats, shaking out the tent poles, too.

WHILE CHRISTIE PUT the poles together, I took the black waterproof bag off the top of the trunk bag and took out the tent and ground cloth.

"Grab the other side would you?" I asked Christie. When we had the ground cloth squared, I tossed the tent over it. Standing on opposite sides, we finished snapping the tent poles together and ran them through the sleeves. Crawling on her knees, Christie tugged on one that hung up on the nylon.

In the twenty times we would repeat the process over the next four months, we never got much better at bending and securing the poles. One of the little buggers always showed a streak of independence, running out on its own before the tent was up.

When we'd won the war of the poles, I shoved the tent stakes in the ground. It was easy in the meadow but on the hard ground that was in our future I'd use a rock as a hammer.

Being much taller than Christie, I tossed the rain fly over the tent and staked it, adjusting the tension while she unrolled the sleeping mats. They were top-of-the-line Thermarest® from REI. Two and half inches thick. We weren't young pups, in fact, well past the age when bodies could comfortably sleep on the ground.

Crawling around setting up camp was hard enough. We'd bought the best sleep mats money could buy.

The mats self-inflated for the most part. A few extra puffs on the valves and they were firm. Christie folded the storage bags in the corner while I tugged the sleeping bags out of their compression sacks and tossed them into the tent.

I left Christie arranging them as if *Sunset* magazine was coming for a photo shoot. I teased her, tossing my camp pillow at her. I wasn't surprised, in fact, I laughed, when it came flying back out of the tent.

When Christie finished her domestic chores, I strapped the tent lamp with Velcro to a loop in the tent, running the cord out the back so it could plug into the bike for power. The bike's auxiliary plug was for riders with electric vests or gloves. While, we didn't have those, it effectively lit a 30-watt bulb.

WHEN WE WERE settled in, we walked back to the office and joined our host for tea.

JUNE 4   I poked my head out of the tent to find a timid blue sky and singing birds. "It's Lisa's birthday," I said to Rick. "I want to find a phone and call her."

He reminded me of the time difference between England and Oregon. "Okay, I'll email if that's all I can do," I said. We ate in the camp's restaurant but they charged for a second coffee. The land of American refills was behind us.

RODE INTO BATH and parked on a circle named "Circus." Matching yellowish-pink stone buildings and hordes of tourists lined the streets.

We joined a tour and learned that a quarter million gallons of 115-degree water pumped through the sacred springs every day. It's thought that the Romans probably occupied Aquae Sulis, the early name for Bath, shortly after their invasion of Britain in AD 43. Where I came from, "old" was 1900s and "ancient" was a hundred years earlier.

THERE'S SUPPOSED TO be a healing quality to the hot springs and I longed to be submerged. Apparently, this wasn't that kind of tour; we minded our manners, kept our clothes on, and stayed harnessed to the group.

AT A COSTUME museum, we paid a small admission fee for a look at 1600s wardrobes. Gave credibility to the phrase, "A picture's worth a thousand words." Back outside, a flute player wearing a powdered wig put on a lively sidewalk concert.

We popped into an internet café to check email at $4 for a half hour. We sent Lisa a "Happy 25th, thinking of you" and Christie quickly disposed of sixteen messages. A message we wouldn't delete was the one she'd sent to herself before we left. She'd explained the idea saying that it would be our brains if all else failed. It didn't cost anything and I had to admit it was pretty smart. Passport numbers, daughter's phone numbers, return flight details, and credit card numbers were listed. Of course, she had a system of swapped numbers so if anyone hacked-in they wouldn't have our data.

I HATED BEING in front of a computer when England was waiting for me so I worked fast. While I was reading, taking notes, and deleting, the woman at the terminal next to us said, "We've had trouble finding computers in some towns, have you?"

I turned my head at the interruption and said without thinking, "We've just started our trip but I think we'll check about twice a month."

"Oh, my." Her voice sounded like hand wringing. "We check almost every day to be sure the kids are OK."

I stared. She looked like she was about my age. I wondered what she'd do if her "kids" were not okay. But I said, "We're on-line now because it's our youngest daughter's birthday." I paused. "She's 25."

Her facial expression said, "Are you nuts or just a horrible mother?"

I went on. "I figure while we're gone, if a parent dies or a daughter gets pregnant, they'll just be more so when I find out."

Laughter erupted across the room. I don't think of myself as funny, and I never tell a joke, but my voice does carry and since I passed fifty, my take on life often brought chuckles that surprised me.

BACK ON THE street, we stopped to watch two acrobats. They wore g-strings and told ribald jokes while doing handstands with lit sparklers in their butts. "Now this is England," I said, applauding. We stood on the sidewalk laughing out loud until the crazy duo moved out of sight.

It was lunch time, so we went into a market in search of a picnic. The carts were tiny. Shoppers were buying just enough for the next two or three meals.

WE CHOSE SANDWICHES. One shrimp, chopped egg, and dill; the other, lox and capers. Not a ham and cheddar in sight. Rick added a bottle of carbonated lemonade and a peach. From the tins on the shelves to frozen goods, all the packaging was new to me. Only the fresh produce was recognizable. I longed to begin sampling and Rick reminded me that since we had a camp stove, I'd have lots of chances to cook.

At check-out, the clerk was seated and customers bagged their own purchases. I happily pulled a string bag from my pack, feeling rather smug at my preparedness, which was actually quite accidental.

We dined on the bank of the Avon River.

IN THE VILLAGE of Wells, we locked our helmets and went into a church that held its first service in AD 909. We headed for Vicars' Close, England's oldest continually occupied residential street. "It's a miracle it survived World Wars I and II," Rick said.

I WAS THINKING the same thing. Wars and bombs, developers with other plans; a wide range of possibilities. I was grateful that disaster had stayed away from this little street so I could fit my feet into the smooth steps, well-worn by centuries of people passing.

In my world, history was confined to school books. But here, connections to the past were part of everyday life. Even the hill where our tent was pitched posted a sign that it was the site of a water mill listed in William the Conquerer's tax book of 1086.

ON TO GLASTONBURY for the hike up the Tor. A mile on a footpath with switchbacks led us up the face of the 600-foot vertical spire where Abbot Richard ordered the hanging of Henry VIII.

In some Arthurian literature, Glastonbury is identified with the tale of Joseph of Arimathea. That story says he stuck his staff in the ground and the hill flowered miraculously into the Glastonbury Thorn, a tree known for blooming twice a year. Whatever. It was a good stretch of the legs and offered up a great view.

The ruins of Glastonbury Abbey dominated the town in the distance. One of the most important abbeys in England, it was the site of the coronation of the King of England in 1016.

Back in Bath, we ate in the campground pub. Lamb, peas and potatoes, washed down with a few pints of Real Ale, a local favorite.

JUNE 5 The tent resisted going back in its bag. Wrestling the damp gear into submission, I thought of a Christmas card my family got every year. I told Rick. "When we were kids, we got this Christmas card from friends of Mom and Dad. It was a tiny sponge. When we soaked it in a bowl of water, the letters grew until it read 'Merry Christmas from the Hambys' in four-inch letters."

Rick looked at me as if the rain had addled my brain. "And the connection is?" he asked with his mouth full of tent pegs.

"Well, fitting everything back on the bike is like putting that sponge back in the envelope," I explained. I had thought my point was obvious.

OUR GEAR DID seem to have grown in just a couple of days but together we managed to stow it. When everything was loaded up, I rinsed our metal coffee mugs and bungeed them to the top of the pile.

THE TALL, DAMP grass made me feel right at home. I could have been in Oregon but I was breaking camp near Bath, England. Pinch me.

I climbed on and we rode toward Wales along miles of tangled streets. Rick navigated by a map tucked into the top of the plastic window in the tank bag. I looked over his shoulder; if Boston maps looked like spaghetti, England was angel hair.

We paused at a roadside pull-out where two elderly couples were having a "boot" picnic. A proper table and chairs were set up and the "boot," or "trunk," was open. Apparently the breeze was too brisk for the ladies, so the men were alone at their table with a pot of tea and the wives sat erect as statues in the back seat of their car. I had to laugh. My British grandmother would have fit right in.

SEVERN BRIDGE SPANS the Bristol Channel and I pulled to a stop at the toll booth. Christie was in charge of gas stations and tolls because it's hard for a motorcycle driver to reach into his pockets. Also, my helmet had a fitted face mask but Christie's could flip up to expose her face if communication was called for. It was a system that worked well except entering Italy but that episode was weeks in the future.

I RODE WITH a flat leather purse in my lap. When I shopped for it at an Arizona department store I'd taken my helmet with me to be sure the strap was long enough. I'm normally not particular about purses but in this case I'd insisted that it not have a flap covering the zipper. Now I was glad for my persistence. I lifted my face mask, took off one glove, tucked it under my leg, unzipped the purse and had my fingers on the coin purse. It was a routine I would repeat often.

MOTORCYCLES WERE FREE. I liked Wales already.

The bridge made a dramatic sweep across the Bristol Channel and suddenly all the signs looked like alphabet soup. I could hear Christie laughing behind me. "These folks need to buy a vowel."

Castles went by in a blur. We'd read in a Rick Steves travel guide about St. Fagen's Welsh Museum and that was our destination. "Museum" sounds like an indoor thing but Fagen's is an outdoor display of Welsh history. Historic buildings were removed from their original sites around Wales and reconstructed on this site. Literally, it's a walk from Celtic times to present day. The centerpiece is a 16th-century manor house on 100 acres.

My favorite was a three-bedroom farm house, circa 1600s, painted red to ward off evil spirits. We wandered for a couple of hours. Native breeds of livestock roamed in the fields.

A MINERS' VILLAGE of six identical row houses was setup with the trappings of the times, 1805–1975. Each looked as if the inhabitants had just stepped out for a moment. Even the gardens were authentic. The earliest had a vegetable garden and sturdy kitchen pottery. The World War II era house had a gas mask hanging from a hook in the kitchen. By the 1970s they had a greenhouse, a VCR, and a quantity of bric-a-brac that nearly forced them into larger homes, a reality we Americans could appreciate.

RIDING IN LIGHT rain, we headed north through Tintern Abbey, still shuddering from the image of the necessary gas mask. Our route followed the bank of the River Wye out of Wales and into Monmouthshire, and we headed to Stow-on-the-Wold. What great names.

The road was about the size of a golf cart path but here they probably called it a sheep trail. It was a good ride until a lorry rounded the corner and nearly tossed us into the brambles. No harm done but after that I was alert, not just watching but listening for oncoming traffic, which only came along every ten minutes or so.

TINTERN ABBEY IS a bombed-out ghostly shell of a once-magnificent church. We rode through the Forest of Dean under a lush canopy of trees that kept us dry. I tipped my head back to stare at the broad green umbrella over our heads, thinking, "Rick doesn't get to see it this way." At least, I hoped he was keeping his eyes on the road. I took off one glove and pulled a tiny journal and golf pencil from my pocket. *"I'm riding through Robin Hood country. It's enchanting but I need a warm shower, food and a walk."* Butts can only take so much cycle riding but being able to take notes in a pocket-size journal helped to pass the time.

STOW-ON-THE-WOLD STANDS ON a 700-foot-high hill at the junction of seven major roads, including Roman Fosse Way. With an ancient cross at one end and the stocks at the other, it wasn't hard to imagine 20,000 sheep at auction on market days at the height of the wool industry.

Christie explored antique shops while I read about the last battle of the English Civil War in 1646. It was a pretty safe bet that she wouldn't buy anything because we didn't have space for more than a postcard.

The Cotswolds are cute on cute so indoor lodging was expensive but Christie looked like she could use a break so I booked a room in a three-room B&B. Our host was a fireman, a good chap. I rationalized the expense; if we went over budget we'd find jobs when we got home.

I WAS ASTONISHED that Rick agreed to the nightly tariff but he's a smart man and a happy wife helps make a good trip. We pulled what we needed from the bike and stuffed it in laundry bags. With the mesh sacks slung over our shoulders and helmets over our arms, we climbed the narrow staircase.

A huge bath tub with a skylight overhead was a welcome sight. While I soaked in bubbles, Rick changed from his leathers and left the room, returning with a bottle of wine and glasses. Sipping wine in the tub, I vowed not to complain; a little misery made pleasure more delicious.

Dressed in non-cycle-riding clothes we walked to dinner. I wrote in my journal, *"A mug of foamy topped Guinness and a bowl of shepherd's pie ends a good day."*

> *"The great French Marshall Lyautey once asked his gardener to plant a tree. The gardener objected that the tree was slow growing and would not reach maturity for 100 years. The Marshall replied, 'In that case, there is no time to lose; plant it this afternoon!'"*
>
> – JOHN F. KENNEDY

CHAPTER 4

COTSWOLDS TO CAERNARFON

JUNE 6   A full English breakfast of bacon, ham, sausage, grilled tomato, fried egg, fried toast, juice and coffee was a heavenly, but decadent, way to start the day. I suggested that maybe we should walk instead of ride after all that food. Two laps around the block and we suited up for the ride to Blenheim Palace.

SHUFFLING TOWARD THE Palace with a pack of just-off-the-bus tourists, I recognized him from the brochure photo. It was the 11th Duke of Marlborough at the wheel of his Land Rover. I halted the tourists like a traffic cop and he waved "thank you." The teenager in the passenger seat smiled but our fellow travelers didn't seem to notice. They just looked annoyed at having to wait a moment. Seeing the Duke and his son was as close as they would probably come to a memorable story from their trip. And they missed it.

Nothing prepared me for the sheer scale of Blenheim. Three acres of roofline would definitely give a guy elbow room when the in-laws visited. We gawked at priceless antiques, tapestries, and paintings of the Duke's ancestors. Touring the rooms where he lived with the Duchess and their children, we saw current family photos displayed on tables. It was opulent but I wouldn't want to live there. I'd get lost trying to find the kitchen.

OUR GUIDE DRONED on with details we needed and more that we didn't. The front doors weighed one ton and the key two and a half pounds. "Is that why the Duke and his family need staff?" I stage whispered in Rick's direction. He didn't answer.

"She said the key weighs more than two pounds!" I said.

"That would definitely work a hole in your pocket," Rick said, gesturing for me to be quiet.

We learned that the library is the longest room in any private home in the world and had more than 10,000 books on the shelves, most printed in the 1800s. Traveling on a motorcycle, my access to books was limited, so the sheer numbers intrigued me.

At the end of the tour, we were released to explore the grounds, two thousand acres of lakes and gardens. "Whew, being inside with a group drives me nuts," I said needlessly to Rick because he knows me so well.

"I could tell it bugged you. But all that Chinese porcelain was pretty amazing," he said.

"My favorite was the hand-painted ceilings and carved cornices. They looked like Wedgwood china. And how about that dining room?" I continued. "A table for thirty-six would make one heck of a Thanksgiving spread, don't ya think?"

He laughed. "You're right about that but a staff of two hundred would be a bit overwhelming."

"Okay. Let's not be British royalty," I said. We walked hand in hand across the lawn, past a waterfall, and back to Woody.

We rode through the Cotswolds, past sunny-yellow stone houses and garlands of clotheslines. The hanging laundry looked to my imagination like silhouettes of the people living inside. Dark trousers, flowered shirts, white sheets. They flapped in the breeze between stucco walls, one after the other. And on the ground, plum cabbage roses and purple irises looked haphazardly clumped and appropriately scruffy. "That's why they call it an English garden," I mused from my comfy backseat. I made a vow to string a clothesline and to try to maintain an unplanned garden when we had a home again.

OUR ROUTE HAD looked intuitive when I studied the map over coffee but now I was completely confused. The twisting unmarked lanes didn't match anything on the map. It might as well have been a maze. I decided it was a good day to ignore the map. We'd end up wherever the road took us.

Burton-on-Water, Upper Slaughter, Lower Slaughter, from Guiting Power to Winchombe. Time seemed to have stood still for these ancient Saxon boroughs. They ranged in size from just a cluster of a half dozen granite cottages to a real town with a church, bank, and shops. They resembled each other, and as Christie pointed out, they looked a great deal like pictures from children's books. We rode slowly, flanked by speckled sheep. Through Sudeley Castle, Stanway, Snowshill, Broadway and Moreton-in-Marsh. But Chipping Camden won my Oscar for best cute-quaint-thatched of the Cotswolds.

BLACK-FACED LAMBS WORE matching black socks and we shared the road with them. Low walls of tumbling rocks meandered across the fields in crooked lines. Robert Frost's poem came back to me.

Something there is that doesn't love a wall,
That sends the frozen-ground-swell under it,
And spills the upper boulders in the sun,
And makes gaps even two can pass abreast.

I was an English teacher and had led hundreds of teenagers through the verses. Seeing the jumbled rows of rocks in the fields now, I had one of many "Aha" moments. It just took being here.

Good fences make good neighbors ...
Something there is that doesn't love a wall,
That wants it down.' I could say 'Elves' to him.

And I would have been a better teacher if I'd been here earlier in my life.

I STOPPED AT a road house for lunch but the kitchen was closed. "Sorry old boy, how 'bout a cold roast beef an' a spot o tea?" Sounded like a good lunch to me but for $15? We were trying to be on a tight budget but sharing a bit more American cash with the Brits than intended seemed like an okay thing to do occasionally. Besides, I was hungry.

I hate to tell this part and Christie pointed out that it wasn't even in my log. But it did happen. Passing through one super cute town Christie asked me to turn around so she could see it again. Being the kind of guy who's got a wife willing to ride through Europe on a motorcycle, I stopped in the narrow lane to turn around. I walked it backward, got a little off-center and we listed to the right. Gravity took over and we went down. It wasn't a crash but it did spread both of us out on the grass and gravel.

I crawled out but Christie didn't. Good news was, she was laughing!

"My foot's stuck," I said with my face in the grass. The motor was still running and Rick bent to lift the bike to free my foot from underneath.

"No," I yelled, "the other one." My left heel was caught on the foot peg.

When Rick realized that it was the foot in the air that was caught, he walked around, pulled my heel loose and I rolled away. Rick helped me up and we checked ourselves for injuries. We'd gone over so gently and landed in grass. Except for a slight pain in my left ankle and Rick's ego, we were unscathed.

Rick turned off the motor and we stood next to Woody wondering how we were going to lift it. Fortunately, the ground tilted in our favor. We crouched down and lifted. When it was part way up, Rick shoved our soft-sided bags underneath, went around to the other side and pulled. When Woody was upright we kissed and climbed back on. Riding a motorcycle with a loved one requires a sense of humor.

We passed "footpath" signs marking a network of one-person-wide trails cut in the fields and over the hillocks. They crisscrossed private land and by local statute, access was open to the public but would revert to the landowner if the path wasn't walked, or rambled, at least once a year. The Rambling Society made sure they were walked. How cool is that?

It was getting late. At a grassy triangle near a tall stone cross stood an old farmhouse. The sign said, "Lodgers welcome." "Why not?" I thought and turned in.

"Where are we?" Christie asked when I stopped in the gravel driveway.

"I have no idea," I said, "but let's see how much they want for a room."

"Jolly good idea," she said, climbing off and removing her helmet.

"How's that ankle?" I asked.

She limped across the driveway but gave me a thumbs-up.

The lodger price was quite reasonable and so was dinner at a locals hang-out. Fish and chips for me, steak and kidney pie for Christie, and a bottle of French wine. Not the expensive California stuff but an authentic $2 French. Retired to the room to watch BBC comedy and news. We're not in Kansas anymore.

JUNE 7 Tasty English breakfast of bangers and eggs and we packed up to ride to Stratford-on-Avon. Turned out to be an overly commercial ode to Shakespeare. Sorry, William, too many post card shops.

Headed northwest on the expressway. Riding two up, at 70 mph, heavily loaded, on the left, had me on edge. And that speed was for the slow lane. We buzzed through Coventry, bypassed industrial Birmingham and into Telford. A sign warned of "loose chippings." Without knowing what they were, images of sliding and tipping came to mind. I didn't think it was possible to concentrate harder but I did.

Other signs that needed translating at first but still made me laugh: "Rumble strips" were speed bumps, of course. "Give way" meant "yield." A "diversion" was a "detour."

I exited at a modern shopping center plastered with familiar logos. McDonald's, Kentucky Fried, Staples. A bright blue and yellow Blockbuster store, Texaco and a Safeway. Christie wasn't amused that we'd gone to so much trouble to essentially be back in the U.S. but I was the one who'd been concentrating on which lane to drive in and I was ready for something familiar. I happily parked in the Burger King lot and we ordered Whoppers for a whopping $5 each. Not the meal, just the burger. And no free drink refills, either.

THE PLACE WAS crowded and a British couple suited up in cycle gear motioned for us to join them. They were Londoners out for a day ride. Chatting with them, I learned that a hamburger bun was a "bap." I didn't need this information but it gave foreign input to Rick's BK stop.

Despite being where English was spoken, there were language differences. Things we rent were "hired."' The beach was the "'strand." Advertising was simply "advert," and a sweater was a "jumper." A "good time" or "good idea" was expressed as "brilliant" or "quite," pronounced "qwat." My favorite was calling a senior citizen an OAP, Old Age Pensioner. The honesty in that phrasing cracked me up. We Americans try so hard to be politically correct.

RIDING OVER MT. Snowdon and down to the sea in Northern Wales, our speed dropped from 70 to 25. The landscape changed from a sprawl of 1950s grey industrial complexes to rolling green hills and cliff-hanging castles. I loosened my grip and began to relax.

At the slower pace, I could make out people hanging off the cliffs. Below the rock climbers was a line of hikers. A large sign told us we were entering Betws-y-Coed, near Snowdonia National Park. There were more bicycles now than cars and the riders looked to be well over sixty. A good omen, as we were rapidly approaching that number ourselves.

We inquired about a camp spot and an English chap with a round hat and equally round Hirohito glasses overheard Christie making a stab at speaking Welsh. This prompted him to launch into a half-hour discourse on Welsh history. He enthusiastically told us of the near demise of the Welsh language and explained how it was making a comeback. While I appreciated his enthusiasm, the sun was getting low and we had a tent to pitch somewhere down the road. We excused ourselves as politely as possible from his monologue.

THE CAMPGROUND WAS called "Coed Helen." I knew that *Coed* was Welsh for "trees," but the campground wasn't in the trees. It was close to a waterfront castle, which was better than trees as far as I was concerned.

A quick toss of the ground cloth and we set up the tent, changed shoes, and walked back to town. The sky was the color of charcoal and a light rain fell around us like a shawl. We grocery shopped for breakfast and lunch and headed back.

It was after midnight but we were so far north that it wasn't dark. I lay in my sleeping bag, thinking about the house we didn't buy in Sedona. For now, "home" was the tent until we packed it and moved on, at which point the cycle became "home." Home wasn't a street address. It was where we parked Woody.

I rolled over and picked up a pen. *"Tonight, my home is a tent next to a castle in Wales. I'm happier than I've been since the girls were toddlers and hugged my neck. I used to think that my happiness would get bigger if I had a larger house in a nicer suburb. Boy, was I wrong."* I closed the journal and shut my eyes. Listening to Rick's gentle snoring, I thought, "Funny how time and experience change what's important."

JUNE 8 I dragged myself out of the tent and assembled our camp stove. It was about the size of a can of beans. I headed for the shower and filled the pot with water for coffee. When I returned, I hooked up the propane and put the water on to boil. With a scoop of instant coffee in each of our stainless cups, we had a cup of morning joe, even if it wasn't very good.

While Christie sliced fruit, rolls, and cheeses, I studiously chose the right spots for my England and Wales stickers.

After breakfast, I bundled our laundry off to the camp building labeled "WASH." But "doing the laundry" wasn't as intuitive as one might think. First, I had to get the bugger to start, a mystery of inserting coins and button pushing. Turned out that the washer washes, nothing more. Spin is a separate feature and costs more. It was complicated and the British dryer took forever. The clothes took a thumping of greater proportions than if I'd pounded them on a rocky river bank.

WHEN THE LAUNDRY finished its strange cycles, we walked, hand-in-hand, to town. Around the yacht club, across a swinging bridge, and through the gates of Caernarfon Castle. Climbing in and out of turrets, we played like eight-year-olds, peering through the slits, ready to shoot an arrow at advancing troops.

We stopped at a barber shop and Rick got a #5 buzz cut that he hoped would cure his helmet-flattened hair. Blow dryers and hair gel weren't possible.

Lunch was pâté, white cheese, and crackers from my pack on a bench outside the castle wall followed by a foamy dark beer in a pub. The pub was something right out of Tolkien. A quiver of fishing rods hung over the stairs and windows overlooked the river. I let myself roll the centuries back.

AT 10:00 P.M. I ducked into the empty laundry room to write in my journal because it had a chair. When we planned the trip, we weren't aware that camp sites would rarely have tables or benches. My middle-aged body was resisting life at ground level.

I VISITED WITH our Dutch neighbor while Rick wrote in his journal. I liked her tent. It had separate areas for kitchen, dressing, and sleeping. We couldn't carry a tent that big but we could certainly improve on what we had. Rick and I had despaired about ours and planned to buy a new one as soon as possible.

JUNE 9   In the wee hours of the morning, rain hammered the thin nylon tent and won. But the misery of a puddle at our feet was nearly negated by a beautiful sight. Through the open tent fly was a sunrise that looked like cotton candy.

It was break-camp-morning but before I was ready to greet the day, Rick reached over and unscrewed the valve on my Thermarest®. The air slowly leaked out and made an unattractive farting noise. Not my favorite way to wake up but Rick found it amusing.

While we had coffee, showered, and got dressed, the Thermarests® self-deflated, as designed. One at a time, Rick kneeled on them, forcing out the rest of the air and rolling them tightly so they could fit back into their bags.

Standing on opposite sides of the tent, we folded the wet rain fly. Or tried to. We never did figure out who was in charge of two-man jobs like folding the fly and ground cover. Rick preferred Air Force precision and I was more a roll-it-up kind of a gal. We stretched the fabric between us and flipped it end-over-end with the objective of making it as small as possible. Somehow we managed but it was never harmonious.

While I rinsed our breakfast dishes, Rick pulled out the tent stakes. We lost a few during the trip but found replacements along the way.

SUITED UP TO ride, I took off my glasses and pulled on my helmet but putting my glasses back on, I bent the hinge on the right side. It was a tight fit and both of us had bent our glasses frames already.

Christie carried a repair kit and she worked for a few minutes before handing them back to me saying, "That's the best I can do. We should stop at an optometrist's office when we see one." I nodded in agreement, slowly working the ear pieces into place.

We rode across the bridge and past Beaumaris Castle on Isle of Anglesey. It even had a moat. And I thought those were only in books.

It was just 75 miles to the ferry landing but the rain had returned so it seemed further. We stopped for gas and I did my normal routine of checking the tire pressure. Nothing new there. I checked it every couple of days. I usually lay on the ground to fit the gauge on the valve but I didn't want to lie in a puddle so I tried the maneuver standing up. Big mistake. Lifting the front to rotate the wheel so I could reach the stem, I grabbed the fender and it snapped off.

"#!@#!@%@." Avoiding Christie's expression of horror, I dug in the bags for a bungee cord. My wife was trusting me to propel us safely across Europe so she probably expected better judgment.

"After two decades of marriage she should know better," I muttered. Fuming, I laid the chunk of red fiberglass on the top of the rear bag and bungeed it snugly. My gloves were soaked and cold rain drops ran down my neck. A wet cat would have been in a better mood.

"IS WOODY'S SNOUT going to perch like a crown for the whole trip?" I asked when I should have kept quiet.

"Just until I can get it re-attached," Rick huffed, getting back on quickly, which avoided further discussion.

I didn't see a purpose for it anyway, other than giving Woody a name. No harm done as far as I was concerned. But Rick's mood matched the weather. After an explosion of swearing, and a sarcastic spate of "Oh that's great. Just what I wanted. Isn't this perfect," he didn't speak. Wouldn't speak.

It was times like this when his good and bad sides collided. Rick's strong, athletic, and quick to action. That makes him a great racquetball player, fun to live with, and an excellent driver. But damn hard on the equipment.

Heading for the ferry, I crouched low, trying to hide from the rain. Dark, low clouds hid any scenery. My hands were wet and cold, which matched my feet and outlook, too. What I could see looked like the Oregon coast. Soon, very soon, I hoped we'd put the foul weather gear deep in the Jesse bags and Rick's foul mood with it.

AT HOLYHEAD TERMINAL we sloshed to the Stena ticket office and chose the slow boat. Three hours to Dublin instead of one but cost $50 less.

"There are only two ways to live your life. One is as though nothing is a miracle. The other is as though everything is...."

– ALBERT EINSTEIN (1879–1955)

CHAPTER 5

RAW, RUGGED AND CHARMING

IRELAND IS HALLOWED ground for golfers. Even though I wasn't planning to play, it was enough to perk a bloke right up.

We rode through Dun Laoghaire and Dalkey in search of a B&B. Actually, we rode through Dalkey twice because Maeve Binchy, an author Christie likes, hails from there so she wanted a repeat.

Didn't see any rooms for rent and it was getting dark so we gave up on the idea of indoor lodging and searched, instead, for a campground. At last, we found camping with a large community table and we were lucky that our table mates didn't mind when we took over the space like a drying room. Wet jackets, helmets, and gloves took what might have been construed as our half. Christie asked if it was okay for us to spread out on the rest of the table and they agreed. They even gave us a map of Holland and advice about what to see when we got there.

I wrote in my journal: *"We have a table. Luxury. A picnic dinner and a bottle of wine. New friends to chat with. Life is good."*

JUNE 10   We awoke to sunshine and green hills. Ireland! Had camp coffee, which Rick was delighted to be able to make using the table instead of on the ground, orange juice, and a sturdy loaf of bread made with Guinness and cherries. Leaving our rain soaked riding gear on the table, anchored by rocks, we walked into the town of Shankill to catch the train to Dublin.

O'CONNELL STREET WAS a good place to begin. It's Europe's widest urban street and home to the infamous Post Office where the Irish Republic freedom cry began in 1916. The battle lasted a week. We had one day to absorb it all.

A HOP-ON-HOP-OFF DOUBLE-DECKER bus tour looked like a good way to make the most of our time. First stop was Trinity College. A Shakespearian actor was our guide. Sporting a blue polka dot scarf, a four-day beard, sunglasses and a black trench coat, he brought history to life like a stage play.

Our little group streamed by the Book of Kells, circa AD 800. The story goes that the manuscript was found by a farmer in 1077. It was written by monks with pens made from goose and swan tail feathers. The paper was vellum from animal skin, stretched and cleaned in lime and lamb excrement. It took 185 calves. Was this guy kidding? I had no idea but it wasn't boring.

Back on the bus, we learned that the mayor of Dublin was a woman. The President of Ireland, too. "Bless their hearts," I thought. In America, we were still bantering about not being "ready for a woman leader."

Our guides plied us with stories about famous Irishmen, too. The list included Jonathan Swift of *Gulliver's Travels*, W.B. Yeats, James Joyce, George Bernard Shaw, and Oscar Wilde. They were proud, too, that *The Messiah* was first conducted in Ireland.

ARTHUR GUINNESS STARTED his brewery in 1759. It was once the largest in the world, producing eight and a half million gallons of our favorite beer every week. A clever bartender drew us each a mug with a perfect shamrock in the dark foam. Does it get better than this? Apparently.

The bus tour was a comedy club on wheels. We passed a pub called "The Cat Dragged Inn" and laughed out loud. The billboards were raunchy and another source of entertainment. An ad for a brand of butter was a photo of a very attractive woman, legs spread, bare feet skyward. It proclaimed, "The healthy spread with a taste for life." Don't think that would cut it on American highways.

JUNE 11 Leaving Dublin, we headed southwest toward Tipperary. I hadn't expected such good cycle roads until the Alps. Plenty of turns and dips with just the right spacing. From the number of leather-clad local riders, it wasn't a secret.

BY THIS TIME, I'd learned to lean into the turns, mirroring Rick's angle. I pretended it was a waltz. And maybe it was.

We stopped for lunch in Shillelagh where Rick asked what the game being played was called. It looked like field hockey.

TURNS OUT, THAT like everything else we'd encountered this side of the Atlantic, it had ancient origins. While Christie headed for the bathroom, I asked some questions. "Hurling's been played for at least 3,000 years," the man told me. "The object is for players to use a wooden stick called a hurley and to hit a small ball called a sliotar. You score by sending the sliotar between the opponents' goalposts. Over the crossbar for one point, under it and into a net for three."

"Sounds a little like hockey or soccer," I replied.

"Ah, no, lad, not that easy," he said. "The sliotar can be caught in the hand and carried not more than four steps." He raised his hand and demonstrated. "Or,'" and he waved what must have been an imaginary stick, "I can strike it in the air or on the ground with me hurley." He was in full animation mode. "It can be kicked or slapped with an open hand for short-range passing." He led me across the crowded pub but when he leapt into the air I thought he'd crash into a bar stool. He was surprisingly agile and I hurried to stay behind him, juggling my leathers and helmet.

"To carry the ball more than four steps one must balance the sliotar on the end o' the stick." He held the menus in front of him as though they balanced a ball on the end. "Or you can bounce it," he continued and I thought of Tiger Woods bouncing a golf ball on the end of a wedge but this guy was not only older than me but working in a restaurant. I thought he was through but he twirled like a star in the musical Rent. With a big grin, he tossed a menu on the scarred wood table. Pulling a chair out for me, and with a gallant gesture, he said, as if in confidence, "The ball can only be handled twice while in possession." With a flourish he slapped the second menu on the table and hurried off.

When Christie joined me, I told her about hurling. "And they don't wear pads but side-to-side shouldering is allowed. These guys are tough." I hadn't seen any helmets either.

AFTER A LUNCH that was more like dinner, we headed out. A crowd had formed near the bike and I was sure that bets were being made on the odds of my lifting my short body onto the tall bike with foreign license plates. Betting was as much a national pastime as hurling. I executed my up-and-over maneuver in true Olympic form. Our audience cheered and men slapped each other on the backs, Riding out of town, Rick waved with one hand; I used both.

RODE THROUGH KILMANAGH, Ballingarry, and Killenaule to Dually and Cashel. "The Rock of Cashel," St. Patrick's Rock, sat on an outcrop of limestone. I came around a corner and it was right there, between the handlebars. We didn't know anything about it but we stopped.

THE CARVED HEAD stones dated from the 12th century but it was the ones with dates during my lifetime that captured my attention. Testimony to widespread war and famine. Tiny headstones brought tears to my eyes. They measured life in months and days.

The only deaths I'd known were my grandparents, at ripe old ages. Our children were in their 20s and healthy. We had been so fortunate.

Rick walked ahead of me and I found him studying the Ryan family plot.

"CHRISTIE, THIS WOMAN lost everyone. Look. Shane. Patrick. Aaron. Cameron. All were just teenagers. And her husband, Ethan, was in his 40s."

"But the mom, Clara, lived to a ripe old 87," Christie said from a few feet away.

OUR WALK THROUGH the cemetery was punctuated by the high, plaintive bleating of lambs on the hillside.

In Tipperary, Rick pulled to the curb in front of a house with a sign boasting "Rooms." Jerry and Dorothy were watching a hurling match on the *telly* and from the quiet streets it was likely that the whole town was doing the same. We quickly agreed on an overnight price and Dorothy pointed up the steep stairs toward our "wash up" room.

We had no idea what a "wash up room" was but we filled our laundry bags with clean underwear, a change of socks and toiletry kits and climbed the stairs to find out. Jerry called after us, "Jes doss about a bit," which I realized from his gestures and inflection meant, "Take it easy."

The room had a bed barely big enough for two, a shelf for clothes and a sink. Lodging with no extras. A "wash up room." Made sense once I saw it. The British and Irish versions of English were pragmatic and honest.

With our belongings stowed, we tiptoed back downstairs to watch Tipperary defeat Cork. It was the first win for the local team in nearly a decade. The four of us celebrated with a pot of tea and Dorothy's *banoffee* pie. She said it was made with bananas, toffee, and thick cream. I could feel the pounds going on but it was delicious.

THEY ASKED ABOUT our travel plans and I said we had a general itinerary but no specifics. Between bites of pie, I said, "We're going to ride across Europe for four months, camping about half the time. We won't ride much more than a couple hundred miles a day and we'll fly home from London at the end of September."

Dorothy was wide-eyed and said she'd never been as far as London.

Jerry said, "You'll need a good purse for all that travel." I just nodded.

Jerry told us about his illegitimate son in America and Dorothy complained that abortions were illegal in Ireland so "5 to 6,000 little Irish blokes die in England every year." Christie looked as though she'd like to be taking notes for a Maeve Binchy novel of her own.

Dorothy owned the florist shop next door and confided about flowers sent and not sent, honorable and not, as though we were best of pals. And it felt like maybe we could be if we stayed long enough.

Leaving Jerry and Dorothy with the dishes, we walked down the steps, into the street, feeling like indulged teenagers. Dorothy called after us, "Now you come home safe."

We turned right and walked a few hundred yards to O'Donovans Pub. The crowd ranged in age from 20 to maybe 90. All were drinking, smoking and foot tapping to a lively guitar.

THE IRISH WE'D seen so far were ruddy cheeked and smiling, with or without teeth. I hadn't seen any evidence that there was much interest in improving one's looks. Not much call for plastic surgeons here, I thought happily.

JUNE 12   I nestled into my cocoon and let Ireland scroll by like a movie. The scenes rolled over Rick's shoulders and helmeted head. Coal faced sheep, old stone churches, black and white cows, cemeteries. Haystacks and hedgerows.

The back roads in England had been mostly two lane with no shoulder but in Ireland they were even narrower. Street signs posted dozens of locations with arrows pointing in every direction. Navigating was pure guesswork but it didn't matter which way Rick turned, we'd arrive together.

With that happy thought, I dozed off for the first of what would be dozens of short naps while underway. I woke up when we slowed down to turn into a gas station. I climbed off and Rick said, "You were dead weight back there."

"Sorry, I took a little nap," I said and left him spluttering about the injustice of it all while I went inside to pay. The shelves were piled high with unwrapped mountains of bread and it smelled like a bakery. Pint jars of home-pickled chutney gleamed on the counter. I bought what I could carry on my lap and promised Rick I wouldn't nap when I had packages in my arms.

IT WAS A stunning ride from Tipperary to Galbally. We shared a platter of toasted goat cheese, tomato and onion sandwiches in a pub. Never thought I'd choose that kind of food but it was better than the hot dog or chili I'd thought I wanted. Even in my late 50s I was finding new favorites. "Good going ol' chap," I thought, giving myself a mental pat on the back.

Killarney was well-outfitted with hotels, shops, and rental carriages. It was a photo-journalist's dream but not what we were looking for so we rode on.

In Kenmare, we found it. Picture-book-perfect, bright blue, red, yellow, and green storefronts and houses. Christie was over the moon.

The campground had an indoor community kitchen including pots and pans. A bakery delivered fresh baked rolls every morning if we ordered the night before. We were sold.

The young campers knew how the stove worked and Christie watched and asked. Coins in the slot gave you thirty minutes for two burners. Those younger gals were good with the stove but our dinner looked better. Decades of cooking gave Christie more experience and she produced a platter of juicy lamb chops, a carrot and zucchini concoction, and fluffy white rice with curry sauce. Give me the older cook any day.

I LOOKED AROUND our makeshift living room while most of the group gave their attention to the soccer game on the small black and white TV in a cabinet. A single German man, a Swiss couple on a bicycle tour, a couple from Belgium, and two gals from Nuremberg whose car had broken down. The roaring fire crackled, adding drawing room charm to the Agatha Christie scene. I'm not a fiction writer but I could imagine that soon the nine of us would be tangled in a complicated plot line, revealing odd bits about ourselves, ultimately revealing the guilty party. Or, more realistically, go on about our separate business in the morning.

JUNE 13   The Ring of Beara is perfect on a bike and less tourist clogged than the better known Ring of Kerry. Traffic was just us and clusters of sheep, splash painted in bright colors. I guessed it was a system of branding but I couldn't be sure.

Rocks on the right. The sea on the left. Through Glengarriff, a postcard-cute town on Bantry Bay, and on to Adrigole and Castle-townbere.

A FILM OF steady rain fell in grey silk threads but the sheep didn't seem to mind. They were adorable, spray-painted in florescent patches of pink or blue and a few miles later in red, then green.

We came out of a tunnel to the sight of a sailboat tugging at her anchor. A carpet of wildflowers surrounded the bay along with a scruffy looking golf course. The ground was impossibly purple, vivid yellow and white. We got off on ground lumpy with rocks but surrounded by fuchsias, hydrangeas, and tree-size rhododendrons. County Cork. I loved the alliteration. Rick headed for the pro shop.

THE NINE-HOLE COURSE cost just $15 to play all day. Number 9 was 165 yards to a small green with water-carry. I had a pang to play but it was raining and we were on a different kind of adventure. I quelled the desire.

WISPS OF WHITE waves looked frosted, their tops blown flat by the cold brine-scented breeze. Bright blue oil drums dotted the bay. We stopped for a cup of hot tea and asked what the drums were for. "The sandy bottom o' the lough is rich feedin' fer shellfish," the pub owner said, pointing toward the window. My gaze followed the length of his arm. A net full of jet black mussels was being lifted out of the icy water. We learned that one bay over was clams. The next, oysters. Then more mussels. A sea stew at our fingertips.

Further around the Ring, a sign read: "Welcome to Allihies, the furthest Irish village from Dublin." I was glad it was lunchtime; my desire to explore went beyond wanting. The colorful storefronts needed closer examination than just passing through.

The rainbow of colors looked as delicious as the foods that came to mind. On my left, a lemon bookstore. Across the street, a blueberry and plum hardware shop and a ruby food market. The church was a whimsical tangerine and butter. O'Sullivans restaurant, mint and lime. A card shop, ladies' dress store, and market lined up in fire engine red, cobalt blue, and bright yellow. Colors from a box of crayons.

WE LOCKED OUR jackets and helmets under the nylon cover. The process had become as automatic as locking a front door.

I made a bee-line for the cranberry storefront, Murphy's Pub. Once we were seated on bar stools near the fireplace, Christie ordered open faced crab toe sandwiches, potato salad with endive, and a pot of tea.

When the starched waiter was out of earshot, I asked Christie, "What's a crab toe sandwich?" She gave me one of her mysterious smiles. "I have absolutely no idea but we'll find out soon."

There was a plaque on the rock fireplace. The place had won a James Joyce award for most authentic pub. "Of course, it had," I thought. It looked like a movie set.

The bartender told us that the bright colors were to contrast with the weather, which was often grey. He also suggested we return on the west coast road through Eyeries.

Following his suggestion, we rode the left edge of the single lane sheep path, and I stayed alert for oncoming traffic. The track with blind corners was actually two way. Wind. Fog. Wet roads. Limited visibility. Narrow winding roads. We stopped often. Christie admired the ocean and mountain views while I gathered my wits for attentive driving.

WE RODE THROUGH milky fog. Stuttering gusts rose off the Irish Sea and the rhythmic thud of the surf beat like a heart against the rocks. Rick honked at every bend, often at 15-second intervals. In the four hours we rode the Ring of Beara we saw just a handful of cars, a few dozen bicycles and motorcycles, and hundreds of black-faced, spray-painted, soot-footed lambs.

At 11:00 p.m. it was still light. I pulled out my journal and pen. *"Our blue tent is too light, noisy in the wind and it leaks. Otherwise, this adventure is wonderful. How can I be so happy when I'm so uncomfortable? Is it the promise of variety? Using a map as a day planner? What I do know is that life is good."*

JUNE 14 Rain had soaked the bottom of my sleeping bag. My feet were wet but not cold. Christie had scooted to the other end of the tent and was curled up and dry. I could smell the fresh bread and I needed to use the bathroom anyway, so I dragged myself out into the rain.

I knew the bakery guy was speaking English but with his accent I didn't understand a single word. Language wasn't necessary. I splashed back to the tent with a paper bag full of fresh rolls. We munched in Christie's dry corner.

THE SHOWER WAS coin operated and didn't have any faucet handles. I wondered if I could shampoo and shave my legs before the water shut off. I gave it a go and finished in plenty of time. After hurrying, I stood under the spray thinking it might never turn off. While the water flowed over my clean body I thought about how not being in control of something as simple as shower water might be good for me.

WE FOLDED THE tent in a quagmire and rode to Avoca Moll's Gap, Ireland's oldest business. They specialized in wool and cashmere clothing made by local weavers with no tax on items shipped to the States but we didn't know what climate we'd settle in, so "just looking" was true.

DINGLE IS FAMOUS for music but the gaily painted shops and pubs made it a delight to look at, too. Rick navigated up a hill to a red and yellow shingled house on John Street. "Mary O'Neil's B+B" the sign read. We took a room and hung our wet camping gear on Mary's clothesline. The music wouldn't start until well past our normal bedtime so we settled in for afternoon naps.

At our first pub, Rick said, "Looks like any place big enough for a crowd can be a pub." This one had been a bicycle store earlier in the day. We joined in the merriment, raising our mugs on cue with our new bar buddies. "*Slahn-chuh* [Sláinte]," we called out, participating in the Gaelic toast to good health.

AT THE SECOND pub, Christie squeezed into a small space on the fireplace hearth and I stood nearby. The place was packed. Between music sets, she said, "It doesn't look like the Irish drink at home." I nodded but the music started up so I couldn't answer. Sure looked like an easy way to entertain your pals with everyone you knew hanging out at the corner pub. But you better be a beer drinker. A shot on the side was common but not a wine glass in sight. And "a beer" meant a pint. Who would want less?

It was nearly midnight at our third pub and the crowd seemed to be just warming up. They sang ballads and roared with laughter. We enjoyed the happy camaraderie but never knew why they were laughing. Just happy I guess. And who wouldn't be? The town of about a thousand residents had fifty pubs.

JUNE 15   Our scrambled eggs and Irish soda bread were delicious. I asked Mary for the recipe. She disappeared into the kitchen and returned with a scrap of paper.

"Sieve in large bowl: 1/2 kg plain flour; pinch each salt, soda, sugar. Scoop handfuls, drop back in bowl to aerate. Add 1/2 liter sour milk."

I realized I was reading out loud when she interrupted. "Quickly. Dah buttermilk and soda 'tis already reacting. An' you'll want ta be kneading lightly; too much toughens an' too little 'twon't rise properly."

The wonderful soda bread was beyond my capabilities but she went on. "Form a round loaf 'bout like this." She made a fist. "Now cu' off the top wit' a floured knife." Her arms slashed the air, loose parts bouncing. "Put at once to bake."

I looked down at the paper. The oven temperature read "Gas mark 8."

The fluffy scrambled eggs were supposed to be easy, too.

"Puh a spaht o milk in dah pan. Add beaten eggs, sal and pepper. Pu a cobr on (ahh, put a cover on it). "Tha's ta secrt." I vowed to try the eggs but made no promises on the soda bread.

Back in our room I did some hand laundry in the sink and Rick squeezed the water out. We hung our underwear and a few shirts on the line next to our tent and gloves.

A BROCHURE IN the room touted the highlights of the Dingle Peninsula, including the "westernmost golf course in Europe." I had every intention of finding it. Heading west on Slea Head Loop, I could hear the bleating of sheep but couldn't see them. The fog was grey cotton glued to my face mask. I hoped the half million sheep on the peninsula knew well enough to stay off the road.

Riding slowly was like taking the motorcycle licensing test. I turned the handle bars instead of leaning to initiate a turn. It required balance and a steady throttle. Christie knew that no sudden movements from the back seat were allowed and that helped.

We stopped to examine an operating 18th-century corn-grinding mill and rode on. The fog lifted and Christie tapped me on the shoulder. We were definitely going to stop again; I'd gotten pretty good at knowing these things.

LORD VENTRY'S MANOR had a sign hanging from a post that indicated it was named for the Goddess of Writing. It was all decked out in palm trees and magnolias and looked out of place. Hedges of bright purple and magenta fuchsias lined the property and a bright yellow manor house sat squarely in the middle. I thought we'd landed on another planet. In a place that gets a hundred inches of rain a year, hence the legendary Irish "40 shades of green," the Lord had blessed this place with heavenly color.

One nice thing about motorcycle travel was that we stopped often because our butts needed a break. Without the ability to wiggle and shift position as we would in a car, we stopped to shake out our limbs almost hourly. As weeks of motorcycle riding turned into months, that aspect didn't change. In a car, we might have cruised along, sightseeing in air-conditioned comfort and missed what we'd come to see.

Now, I breathed deeply and murmured to myself, "Three and a half more months without windows between me and the view. Lovely." A sign read "Taisteal go Mall," which meant "Go Slow." I vowed to take that message with me and breathed deeply, savoring the musky scent of peat.

PERCHED ON A cliff above Dingle Bay at the base of Mount Eagle, Dunbeg Fort sat proudly. It was built in the Iron Age. We were walking backward in time.

Stone igloo-shaped buildings looked intriguing. A motorcycle didn't need much room to park so we stopped. They were beehive huts, called "Ringforts," built by seventh-century monks. After all that time, the piles of loose stones were still sitting there, unguarded and intact. Amazing.

The movie *Far and Away* was filmed on the Dingle peninsula, so we stopped to explore one of the film's sets. In the 1992 adventure-drama, Tom Cruise and Nicole Kidman played Irish immigrants seeking their fortune in 1890s America. We'd seen the movie at least twice but Christie had no memory of it.

BAMBOO RUSHES WERE thick on both sides of the road and it occurred to me that they're used to make the thatched roofs that so many houses still had. Above them, the land pitched sharply, terraced into rows where potatoes used to grow.

On the cliff above a long beach, a view of the Blasket Islands would have been possible except for the fog that hung just a few feet above our heads. We had a picnic on the seawall. Crab sandwiches and ginger fingers. That's what the package said, "fingers," but they were just skinny, bland, soft gingersnaps. The low ceiling eliminated a good view but the air smelled like wood smoke, clover, and the sea.

IT DIDN'T TAKE much imagination to visualize the hard-working Irish picking the stones out of the ground and piling them into fences. They hauled sand and seaweed up the nearly vertical incline to nourish the clay soil. Sixty thousand people were on the peninsula in 1845 but then the potatoes rotted. Down to just 2,500 now.

"The Irish have every reason to shake a fist at the almighty," Christie said.

"But instead there seems to be a national sense of humor. I've heard more full belly laughs here than just about anyplace," I said.

"Maybe they laugh because so much grief has played out on their watch," she said and we climbed back on the bike.

As if proving the point, in Dunquin we passed rock homes that had been abandoned in desperation a century and a half earlier.

At the next overhang, a plaque honored the fact that scenes from *Ryan's Daughter* were filmed there. I've seen a lot of movies but had no knowledge of that one. Apparently Christie did. She transformed into someone I hardly knew. She was a hundred yards from me in just moments, waving her arms and skipping as if slightly deranged.

I TUGGED OFF my leathers and tried to imagine I wore a flowing skirt instead of jeans. In a replica of a scene I thought I remembered from the 1970 movie, I threw my hands over my head and ran along the cliff, imaginary long locks trailing in the wind.

When I was through re-enacting the part of Rosy, we clambered down to the beach on steps roughly chopped into the rocks. The face of the cliff above our heads was covered by a mass of black shiny mussels. Sea life that high above the strand was a visible reminder that the tides fluctuated eight to ten feet. Not a safe place to be without an exit route.

The town of Ballyferriter, Baile an Fheirtéaraigh, was established by a Norman family in the 12th century. It had three pubs. Tigh Uí Chatháin, Tigh Uí Mhurchú and Tigh an Tsaorsaigh, The only hotel was Óstán Cheann Sibéal. Rick stopped long enough for me to copy the spellings. While I was writing the names, he played with possible pronunciations of the impossible names.

"I'll be stoppin' fer a pint at Tie Goo Chat but if I'm not there look for me at Murchu or Soar Say."

I shook my head in amusement. "I know that's not how they say it."

"It's sure a language with interesting letter combinations, though," Rick said.

We were laughing but Gaelic did make menus and maps hard to interpret.

OUR CIRCLE DRIVE was nearly complete and we hadn't seen the golf course. Circling back a few miles, I saw the sign. "Galfchúrsa." Of course! How had I missed it?

I checked on renting clubs. We carried a small zip-lock bag with golf gloves, a dozen tees, and markers. We would wear motorcycle boots and fortunately, the gas stations were offering a sleeve of cheap balls as a promotion and I'd already stashed a few.

Christie kept a list of random golf courses we'd played while traveling. Adding Ireland seemed like a good idea, especially at a little course. I'd save the big boys until I came back with proper shoes and my own clubs.

THERE WERE MORE sheep than golfers on the eighteen-hole track with its thick tufts of turf and deep trough sand traps. The score card was in Gaelic.

Two young men joined us for the last few holes. They had just finished their "leaving certs," an Irish test that determines which university they'd attend. They were hopeful and "shedding pent up nerves with a bit o the golf."

Walking back to the bike, I said, "This place has a sense of timelessness."

"Sure does," Rick replied. "Golf was supposed to be played this way."

Back in our room, I re-read the directions to the course. "Once the golf traveler sees nothing in any direction except mountains, the Atlantic Ocean and the rocky buttes that rise from it, and the wide, fresh sky, is Ceann Sibeal Golf Course." No wonder it was hard to find.

JUNE 16 The breakfast room at O'Neils had been overrun by three couples, embarrassingly American. Brash and boisterous, too big for the room. I wrote in my journal: *"It's so unseemly to take over a space with your voice, belongings and big movements. Makes me apologetic, embarrassed and quieter. My countrymen come to see but make so much noise they defy the experience to penetrate. Ouch."*

Leaving colorful little Dingle cradled in the valley, we rode up and out of the fog to Conor Pass. At the top was a wide space, appropriately called a "car park." Rick pulled in next to a bike exactly like ours, only lime green.

In the clearing, a harpist played and a rainbow appeared. Were we in heaven?

WE TOOK OFF our helmets and shrugged out of our jackets in complete silence, awed by the surprise of a man sitting on a little stool making beautiful music on a harp. He wore a tiny green felt cap with a tall feather, a rumpled white shirt and a red bow tie, a comical combination.

The folks on the green BMW were Paul and Carol from a London suburb. We chatted while the harpist played. They offered that we should stay at their house when we returned to England. That seemed a long way off but we kept their contact info.

When we said good-bye to Paul and Carol and the heavenly music, we rode toward Brandon Bay. The day had turned warm and we passed cliffs, a waterfall, and lakes. Slowed down through the town of Castlegregory and made a note to return someday. It checked all the boxes: golf, a beach, and lodging.

Ballybunion is famous for golf but the first thing we saw in town was a larger-than-life statue of Bill Clinton. I thought he probably came for the golf but called it a political outing. Whatever the nature of his trip, the local folks were clearly pleased he'd been there.

The course was closed in preparation for the Irish Open, which saved me the mental angst of wanting to play. We walked four of the holes on the Old Course. Huge blind shots over the ocean. Impossible beach grass thickets waiting to snatch the errant shot. Looked like it could bring a decent golfer to his knees.

Chose a "take away" lunch and ate our burgers on a bluff. A sign in Gaelic read, "Cead mile failte," which meant, "A thousand welcomes." I felt sufficiently welcomed.

AT THE SHANNON River, we rode straight onto a departing ferry. Our timing was so perfect it was more like riding across a bridge than catching a boat. What made it even more ludicrous was that we hadn't even known a river was there.

On the short ferry ride, I said to Rick, "I think one difference between a traveler and a tourist is the willingness to be surprised."

"Could be," he said. "Tourists don't have time for surprises. Travelers do." After a pause, he added, "I like being a traveler. Except when being a tourist is easier," and laughed.

I had to laugh, too, but I steeled myself for the inevitable surprises that might not be so serendipitous. Every day, Rick bungeed the bike's broken red snout on the bike. I hoped it would be our worst mistake.

The ferry ride was just twenty minutes. We followed the road north. All around us, mossy green fields were stitched together by rows of rock walls and heather hedges. It looked like a big green quilt. The next town was Quilty. Was I reading that right?

THE CLIFFS OF Moher rise 700 feet above the Atlantic Ocean. A path led out to Hag's Head and we hiked to O'Brien's Tower. It was built by Sir Cornelius O'Brien to impress female visitors. We climbed to the top of the watchtower for a view of the Aran Islands and Galway Bay. Okay, O'Brien, Christie's impressed.

In Doolin it wasn't hard to choose lodging. The whole town was about as long as two par fives.

AT THE BAR, an old man beamed at us, creasing his dark skin into a thousand tiny rivers. Some front teeth were missing, so when he smiled it looked like he had white goalposts in his mouth. I was so fascinated by his appearance and enthusiasm that it was hard to concentrate on what he was saying.

HE TOLD US that the Irish government encourages that Gaelic be spoken and where it is, they call it "Gaeltacht." This proud country was losing its language but now lots of signs were in Gaelic with the old Irish lettering. That made using an English language map an especially bad idea, which we'd already learned.

Dinner was the best Irish stew so far, followed by lively music at O'Conners Pub.

JUNE 17 After breakfast, we headed out but got lost. Intersections had signs but the arrows stuck out like spokes on a wheel and, of course, most were in Gaelic. Finally, a gas station attendant pointed us in the right direction.

In Knock we got off just to rest our butts. When I learned that nearly a half million pilgrims visited annually, I had to accept that it might not be as hard to find as I'd made it. Apparently, the Virgin Mary and St. Joseph appeared in 1879 and that's all it took to get on the map. I could think of some dying American towns that could benefit from that line of marketing.

Between Sligo and Donegal we happened on the grave of W.B. Yeats. With an English teacher riding behind me it was an obvious stop. We walked across the cemetery, following the signs to Yeats' resting place.

RICK WON BIG points for noticing and turning in to take a look. But lost them when we left and nearly joined Yeats at six feet under. For the very first time, he reverted to American driving habits and looked the wrong way. I screamed. He heard me. We lurched to a stop.

MOST OF A motorcycle's braking is on the front wheel so when I hit the brakes the nose dove forward and we stopped quickly. No harm was done other than a hammering pulse and Christie complaining of slightly damp pants.

BEFORE LEAVING ON the trip, we'd set up a system that was supposed to help us stay safe. Before we ventured into traffic, Rick would say, "Ready?" Since "No" sounded like "Go," I'd decided on "Clear." That had been our routine but the close call at Yeats grave made it clear that screaming works, too.

WE RODE TO Sligo, which looked interesting and Christie had a sudden urge to collect seashells. After six years on a sailboat, one thing we didn't need was more seashells. She's a logical gal and was easy to convince. But, honestly, I could see why she was tempted. Sligo's Irish name, Sligeach, means "shelly place."

COMING OUT OF the Tourist Information office I thought I'd walked into a costume party, nearly colliding with an enormous rose velvet hat that bounced above three strands of pearls. The owner had ruddy cheeks and heavy eyebrows. She was followed by a brigade of about a dozen similarly attired wide women.

"Excuse me," turned into a conversation. They were going to a wedding. Even though her accent was thick, at least we shared vocabulary. The journalist in me loves to ask questions. "Whatever will I do to satisfy my curiosity in Denmark, Germany, Austria, Italy, and France?" I thought, as her friend bounced by, encased in a shiny pink dress that looked like patent-leather. I felt woefully out of place in black leathers.

IN ARDARA AND Maas "tent pitching" wasn't allowed so we continued to Portnoo. Bought wine, bread, and pâté for dinner; yogurt and two bananas for breakfast. The provisions rode on Christie's lap. On to Dungloe.

ROCKS SHAPED LIKE a table and chairs sat right next to our camping space. It was a little Flintstone-esque but I clapped my hands in delight. Dining for six!

Our neighbors were French and spoke no English. The four of us tried gestures and we spread out a world map to show where we were from. They were vacationing in a tiny dollhouse of a trailer they called a "caravan." It looked like a compressed Airstream Bambi and when they offered us a look inside, that's all we could do.

We walked into town for a draft of Guinness and a shot of Powers while England beat Germany on TV. It was soccer to us but they called it "football." Whatever its name, it's the world's most popular sport and I could see why. It took about half the time of American football because they didn't have commercial breaks or timeouts. When the game was over, the TV was muted, instruments appeared from under the tables, and the real party began. I liked their priorities.

JUNE 18 Took our laundry to town and sat on a park bench reading a newspaper. An Irish chap named Eugene befriended us. He owned the pub "jes down the way" and at his urging, we followed. It was 11:30 on Sunday morning. Signs said "no minors" and "no liquor service on Sundays." A tipsy father and two young children passed us in the doorway. Apparently some laws were flexible.

Back in the campground, with our clean clothes folded in the tent, we borrowed bicycles. A river ran through the village and we rode along its banks. We investigated the source of some music and found a high school band practicing for a parade. We pulled our sleep mats into the sunshine. With some reconfiguration, the mats became ground level chairs with a back rest but I hadn't tried it yet. I assembled mine but Christie preferred the prone position. I read the *Irish Times* while Christie slept.

IT WAS FATHER'S Day, so I called my Dad. Mom and Dad had been less than thrilled about our trip from its inception.

Dad's objection was that Rick should be working, not playing. Mom's displeasure was partly concern for my safety, which as a mother, I could appreciate. But there was also the simple fact that motorcycle riding came with an image of tattoos and an unseemly wardrobe. The utter absence of pretty clothes and country club good taste must have made her wonder where I'd come from. I shoved that family baggage to the bottom of my saddle bag and tried not to unpack it very often.

Rick's parents were deceased so he had no Father's Day calls to make but we did call the kids. Lisa wasn't home but Rick left a message. We talked to AJ. She and her husband, Chris, were busy with work, she at NBC and he at IBM. Life in Manhattan was good and they hung up just as the prepaid card ran out.

WALKED INTO TOWN for dinner and met a fellow from Glasgow, Patrick Doyle. He bought us a pint and asked if we would send him a postcard from America and a copy of *Undaunted Courage*, which I did when the trip ended.

RICK'S NEW FRIEND joined us for dinner. I ordered "carvers," a platter of meat, potatoes, and vegetables. Eating my dinner and listening to the guys talk, I was shocked when Patrick, without a word to me, reached across the table and actually ate food off my plate. It seemed normal to him.

JUNE 19 Entering Northern Ireland I expected a sign or an International Border crossing. Nothing. The only indication that we'd left the Republic of Ireland was improved roads. Wider and smoother. And the signs were in English, not Gaelic.

In Derry, Northern Ireland, concertina wire gave the buildings a prison-look. Except for the armored tanks sharing the road, it reminded me of the Los Angeles high school where I'd taught. The buildings were appropriately gun metal grey.

We saw signs marking the spot where British paratroopers opened fire on civilians in 1972, killing thirteen unarmed demonstrators in what became known as Bloody Sunday. That year, I was giving birth to our first daughter, Amy Jean. I'd been young, distracted, and embarrassingly naive. Belatedly, I paid attention to Irish history.

The coastline was rugged. A short walk took us across park-like grounds to the ruins of a 1776 mansion, built for the Anglican Bishop of Derry. Gutted by fire and left to decay, it was still an impressive ruin. It looked quite sophisticated for having been built back when America was just drafting the Declaration of Independence.

A bit further on, we explored the Mussenden Temple. It sits just a few hundred feet above the ocean and has four openings, three windows and a door, that exactly face the compass points. Apparently it was a library once, but local legend has it that the Bishop's mistress used it as a boudoir. Pretty engaging stuff.

Stopped where a cluster of caravans were parked to see if we could pitch the tent. A British chap, a sheep farmer, told us it was illegal to camp but "by the time it gets to the courts, you'll be gone." We just couldn't make ourselves do it.

Through Portstewart into Portrush. The Irish Amateur was underway at Royal Portrush, another highly rated track in golf world rankings but we rode on and found camping in Portballintrae. We pitched the tent next to a tall fence that made a handy windbreak.

Fog rolled down the moor, creeping through the trees. It muffled sound and covered the low-lying ground with a thick grey blanket. We camped next to a row of wind-bent stumps on an outcropping just south of the 13th-century Dunluce Castle, an impressive ruin. The story goes that during a storm in 1639 the whole kitchen, complete with the cooks and dinner, fell off the cliff.

CHRISTIE WAS HORRIFIED by the ghost story for cooks. I assured her I wouldn't expect dinner cooked on a cliff and we walked to Sweenies Public House for steak and Guinness pie chased down by more Guinness.

JUNE 20 It was a short ride to the Giant's Causeway, a National Heritage site. An estimated 37,000 basalt columns jutted out of the sea, some of their shapes resembling castles. In fact, at Chimney Point, the ships of the Spanish Armada once opened fire believing they were attacking Dunluce Castle to the west.

WE GOT AWAY from the crowds by walking along the cliffs. The waves crashed, playing the same song from the days

before people stood there. We passed a fisherman in a yellow rain slicker, a flour sack of fish slung over his shoulder. A swinging rope bridge led to the fishermen's island.

CROSSING A GRASSY field, I slipped and landed in the grass on my back. Christie recorded my fall from grace with her camera. I tried to make it look like I was resting.

Coleraine is the Northern Ireland version of Newport Beach, California. Stately homes, well-tended gardens, tennis courts, and a marina. From there we headed for some serious fun. A tour of the 400-year-old Bushmills Whiskey distillery.

A WOMAN AT the Causeway had told me to volunteer at Bushmills if given a chance. I didn't know what I was volunteering for but when our guide asked for volunteers, my hand shot up. And that's how I became an official whiskey taster.

Seated in front of a paper mat divided into thirty boxes, there were ten shot glasses in a row. The "job"' was to drain

a glass and slide it to a space that indicated whether I'd liked it or not. First were the Irish whiskeys: Powers, Jameson and Bushmills. Our leader explained that the color of the hootch came from the wooden cask, and the smoky flavor was a result of peat-fired processing. I preferred Powers.

Next on my game board was Black Bush, ten-year-old Bushmills, Glenfiddich, Johnny Walker Red, and Jim Beam. It was a shell game for alcoholics and more than I could handle alone so I enlisted Rick's help. He didn't look like he minded but he was driving, so I didn't let him help much and the official Bushmills tasting certificate was mine.

Back at camp, I hung my rain jacket over the handlebar and heard a sizzling sound. The nylon had melted on the hot muffler. The jacket sleeve had a distinctly lacy pattern and the muffler sported the residue. Rick was exceptionally quiet and I looked up but he just smiled and said, "You're gonna need a new jacket."

FIERCE WINDS AND rain overnight. Even the tent pegs pulled loose. The front of the tent collapsed with every gust. Damn American technology. I vowed to buy a European tent at the first opportunity.

JUNE 21 Clear skies greeted us, which was good because it was so much easier to pack when it wasn't pouring. We headed toward Belfast, planning to catch the late afternoon ferry.

Made a tourist stop in Cullybackey at the ancestral home of Chester Arthur.

"Chester, who?" Christie asked.

Arthur was America's 21st president and his parents came from this little town. We toured the cottage with a group of Irish school kids. They treated us like celebrities because we were Americans, like Chester. Sampled soda bread cooked over a peat fire; tasted like our English muffins.

Leaving the president's parents' home, I relaxed into my seat and let my mind float. I'd come to love Ireland. A lush, boggy, fairy-tale place, punctuated with sheep, colorful buildings, and a rugged coastline. Images lined up like postcards and I closed my eyes.

In the week we'd spent circumnavigating Ireland, roads had run like veins across our route. I thought about the children playing in the streets and smiling Irish of all ages waving as we passed. The harp, lyrical language, shades of green and misty breezes. Good memories included more than a few mugs of frothy Guinness and comfort food. We'd sung in the pubs and moved at a leisurely pace. I loved not being in a hurry. Slumping forward against Rick's leather jacket, I almost dozed off.

At Ballymena, I stopped at a Harley store just to look and because we were early for the ferry. Still killing time, I stopped at a 12th-century Norman castle at Carrickfergus, a fashionable suburb of Belfast. In the parking lot, I reached into the tent bag to pull out the nylon bike cover. It wasn't there.

I swore. I yelled. But Christie was calm and asked, "Where did we see it last?" I hate it when she's logical. I'd hung it to dry on the fence at the caravan park. Maybe it was still there.

We had all of Europe to tour and the purpose of the cover was to keep our helmets and jackets out of sight. Being super cheap and not having any idea if we could replace it, back we went in a downpour.

The abrupt change of pace strangled me. "We won't see any of Belfast and we might not be on the ferry," I fumed. This is when motorcycle travel came in handy. Rick couldn't hear me venting.

It was a great relief to see our red and black cycle cover rain-plastered to the fence. I hopped off almost before Rick stopped. Together, we wrung it out as best we could, stuffed it where it belonged, and rode away, still hoping to catch the ferry. Tucked behind Rick to avoid the worst of the rain, I repeated over and over, "No blame, we're a team," and tried to believe it. At 80 mph it was cold.

My helmet air vent must have been open because water ran down my chin. My gloves were sponges and my socks the same. Our leisurely one-way trip had taken 3 1/2 hours. The round-trip retrieval mission was accomplished in just under three. Nice to know we could put the pedal down when we needed to. Got gas and met the Stena Line to Stranraer, Scotland. Barely.

WE TOWEL DRIED our hair, changed socks and spread the wet gear out under the cover, locking it all to the bike. Upstairs, we found a dry and comfy seat with a view for the two-hour trip. Some Guinness and cards and Christie looked less pissed.

"There is nothing about us more human than our curiosity; and there is no way to satisfy that curiosity, short of exploration."

– JEFF GREENWALD,
SCRATCHING THE SURFACE

CHAPTER 6

RALLY AND OLD YORK

"WELCOME TO SCOTLAND," the sign read. Customs was a wave-through. It was 8:00 p.m., broad daylight, and a spectacular waterfront drive up the coast. Lots of caravan camping on the beach but we were ready for indoor sleeping. Christie tapped on my shoulder pointing at a double rainbow that hovered over a rock the shape of a haystack. I glanced, appreciatively, and turned my attention back to the road. We were headed to Ayr, the largest of the Clyde Coast holiday towns, 32 miles southwest of Glasgow. It was easily sign-posted.

At a family-owned inn Christie inquired and "Yes," they had a room and, "Yes," we could park in their garage. We moved in and walked to town for Chinese food and low-priced Scotch cocktails.

JUNE 22 At a supply store in Ayr, I replaced my melted jacket and we bought a better tent. It was taller, had a bigger footprint, rain flaps at the front and rear for undercover storage, and it wasn't too big or heavy to carry. We trusted it wouldn't leak.

Back at the inn we packed up and rode back to the store to pick up the tent. Rick parked at the curb, got off, and the bike tipped over. Normally I got off first but instead, I was lying on the sidewalk. "How glamorous," I thought.

Rick was suitably distressed and helped me up. Assessing that I wasn't seriously injured, he left me to nurse my wounds. My left arm and hip bore the brunt of the fall. I took off my jacket and rubbed my sore elbow.

I APOLOGIZED AGAIN to Christie but she didn't seem to be in a receiving mood. We left the old tent at the shop and I fit the new one in its space. Leaving Ayr, Royal Troon Golf Club beckoned. "Sorry, chap," I reminded myself, "this isn't a golf outing," so we rode on by.

I SAT GINGERLY, it hurt to move. I had known we might have an accident but this was the second time Rick had dumped the bike and I was the only one who got hurt. I knew it wasn't intentional but the moisture now wasn't from rain, it was steam from my ears. Maybe I'd toss him to the Loch Ness monster. We'd be there soon.

RODE ACROSS THE bridge into Loch Lomond. The Loch looked like Lake Tahoe. We detoured into Luss and an exclusive golf course where they wouldn't even consider letting us take a peek. We walked through the village that dated back to at least AD 1300. Actually, I walked and Christie limped. Had Scotch pasties for lunch. Bagpipes played. It was postcard perfect, tour bus stuff. Skirted the Loch Lomond on a smooth, wide, winding road.

CASTLES WERE EVERYWHERE. "Lots of geographic areas have an iconic feature," I mused. In Arizona it's cactus; Canada, waterfalls, but I'd never thought that Scotland would have so many castles crowning its hilltops. *"If just one could be transplanted to Seaside, Oregon, it would change the economy of the entire coast,"* I wrote in my journal.

In Oban, I bought a flask of Scotch just the right size to fit the inside pocket of my leather jacket. I told Rick, "It's medicinal, for injured passengers only."

HAD DINNER WITH an Australian couple who invited us to their house for a country music festival in late January. It wasn't on our travel radar but we shared email addresses just in case.

Went to an American movie and what got my attention was the ads. Some were for liquor and all were ribald. "Never would we see that in America," I thought.

JUNE 23 Word was out that we could expect a "heavy midge," no-see-um, population on the coast so we opted to skip the Isle of Skye in favor of Inverness.

FORESTS OF RHODODENDRONS turned the hillsides purple. The sky was molten but the rain more misty than drenching. It looked like Washington state's Olympic Peninsula dressed in tartan plaid and dotted with castles. Stopped in Fort William and bought a picnic lunch. Onion fritters, curried vegetable pasty, a chicken with corn sandwich and a couple of bottles of carbonated lemonade.

A CONCRETE SLAB in the woods served as a table. The "'picnic rule" was in effect. A proper table appeared around the next bend, right after the meal.

Soon after our picnic, construction stopped traffic so long we got off and struck up a conversation with a fellow BMW rider. Tim was towing a trailer, and his daughter, Jenny, rode in a side car.

His wife, Sue, followed on her own bike. They lived in London and were surprised by our Oregon license plates.

"Are you headed to the rally?" Tim asked.

"No. But we could change our plans. What's it about?" I asked.

"It's for BMWs, up the road at Dornoch. They call it the 'longest day rally' because it's during the equinox," Sue said.

"Sounds good to me," Christie said with a big smile. One of the many things I love about her is enthusiasm. Makes her a darn good life partner.

Jenny must have been about nine and she piped up, "It's really cool. Right on the ocean. All BMWs but I'll probably be the only kid."

So, a new plan was hatched. We'd head for Dornoch and our new friends would meet us there. They were going to Loch Ness first to spy the legendary monster.

At a coffee stop in Tain, Scotland's oldest "royal burgh," I dubbed the area the "Argyle route." The pattern of lakes and sailboats, angled between green hills, had a diamond pattern, I explained to Rick. He just shook his head, certain I was nipping too enthusiastically on my medicinal scotch.

We learned that the last witch in Scotland was burned in Dornoch in 1722. A stone church dominated Dornoch's town center and with a little help we found the area reserved for the rally. It was sponsored by the Scottish Section of the BMW club.

"No," we had not preregistered, I answered the chap at the sign-in table. "Didn't know about it until we were just down the road this morning," I showed my BMW motorcycle club card and that instantly qualified us for free admission.

"Welcome," he said and shook my hand. "Park your bike. Pitch your tent. Have a go at the food and drink."

THE RALLY CAMP site looked across the Dornoch Firth, the Scottish word for a bay or inlet. But we didn't take much time to contemplate it; the wind was coming up. Rick used a rock to hammer the tent pegs into the ground.

A German rider next to us eyed our Oregon plates and was bummed that she wouldn't be winning the "I came the furthest award," but it turned out there was no prize.

With our new Scottish tent set up and neighbors greeted, we walked back to town for wine and food supplies, or, "packets" and "tins," I was told they're called. A hedge of familiar yellow bushes was called "broom." "Aha," I thought as the proverbial light went on. Scotch broom. Scotland. Sometimes I connect dots more slowly than others.

Orange, pink, and plum tufts of wildflowers exploded between the taller yellow broom. Over another hillock, I stumbled on a chambered cairn, relics of the Picts, who lived on the land for thousands of years, until the Vikings arrived and forced them out.

While Dornoch has history, it's now better known for tourist hotels, shops, golf, and weddings. Madonna was married at Dornoch's Skibo Castle and Gwyneth Paltrow was a bridesmaid. We explored the 15th-century castle and the Bishop's Palace. Its manicured gardens had an air of grace retained from bygone years.

DORNOCH WAS TRANQUIL but history tells of prolonged and bloody disputes, political intrigue, and family vendettas, from Viking raids in the ninth century to a Jacobite orgy of looting and burning in 1746.

When we returned to the rally site, there were about thirty tents clustered near ours and a total of fifty by the weekend. Bikers from London, Holland, Germany, and of course, Oregon. The couple we'd met at Burger King was even there.

Our pals from the traffic slow-down arrived and Jenny gave me a six-inch stuffed Loch Ness monster for good luck. Sue demonstrated what is so charming and ribald about English humor every time she spoke. One of my favorites was, "The only time me husband would notice the color o' me hair would be if ah dyed me pubies."

I couldn't resist. "Well did you?" Christie kicked me but she was laughing, too.

"Have a look fo' youself. They're purple now." Just for the record, I didn't look.

We queued up for group pasta, salad, bread, and red wine. Sitting in the tall grass in a circle of new friends, we chatted about our lives.

TIM STOOD TO get seconds on pasta and tripped over a rock. "Bugger it," he said. I loved the new words and started to laugh. Beside me, Jenny, asked. "Are you creasing up inside?" That made me laugh even harder.

JUNE 24 Most of the bikers were "kitted out" for an all-day ride. We rode every day anyway so chose not to go with them. One of our neighbors said, "It's pretty bloody cheeky not to go."

"God, I love the lingo," I said to Rick as the group rode away.

We explored the town where a fair was in full swing. Costumes, bake sales, and a bagpipe band filled the square with energy. In the 13th-century cathedral, an organist was practicing and the sound was pure angels, reverberating off the stone and stained glass.

GAMES OF CHANCE were set up in booths and at another a crew cooked up small pancakes on a griddle. A long line of folks were willing to pay what seemed to me like a large sum for a couple of plain old hotcakes. Not sure what that was about. Maybe pancakes were a delicacy.

Dornoch is, of course, also home to the Royal Dornoch Golf Club. It's not only in the world's top twenty and the most northerly, it's also third oldest in the world, having been first played in 1618. Old Tom Morris, one of golf's most famous architects, was born in Dornoch. I was determined to have a go at the links but Christie begged off. She said it wasn't because of the fall in Ayr but that she'd rather spend her greens fees shopping later in the trip.

JUNE 25   Rick's golf day dawned grey, windy, and cold. Our fellow bikers were up early to return to London, Belfast, and the continent. I planned to attend a Scottish church service. Rick and I walked together as far as the fork, where he turned right on the golf course road.

"Have fun, honey," I said.

"You too. And pray that I don't run out of balls in the gorse," he chuckled.

I RENTED CLUBS and dropped my free-at-the-gas-station balls into the bag. The starter introduced us as "Mr. Dooley meet Mr. Gorsline, from America. He will be joining you today."

I wore muddy boots, motorcycle rain pants and an oversized windbreaker because it was big enough to fit over my leather jacket. Roger was from a private club near London. He was tall and slender and nattily attired in grey slacks, a black and grey argyle sweater, and shiny black Footjoys®.

We may have looked like the odd couple but by the twelfth hole, when I was 3-up in our friendly match, Roger asked me join him in the clubhouse "for a pint and a wee taste of the whiskey."

I SAT IN the back pew at the Dornoch Free Church of Scotland. There were about forty of us, mostly age eighty-plus with another handful under age ten and not much in between. I surveyed the group and saw lots of plaid jackets and 1950s hats. They looked typecast by Hollywood. Downturned mouths and ruddy cheeks. The ancient minister looked as if he might tip over and go with the angels at any moment but he kept breathing and piously preached to his flock. I had the irreverent thought that if he changed languages, or died, his congregation would stay squarely in position until directed to leave. My thoughts were more spiritual at the ocean's edge, in a field of wild flowers or gazing at a green field dotted with sheep than seated on a hard pew.

The scripture leader was another truly ancient gent who sang the Psalms instead of reading, as I was used to. Despite his dour expression, each note was delivered with the purity of a single key on an organ. The tone reverberated with perfect pitch through the small sanctuary but the flock remained unmoved. I happily fled to the cobblestone street as early as possible.

In a pub on a side street I had a solo lunch of baked camembert with currant jam and red wine since they hadn't offered communion at church. It was odd having lunch alone. This was the longest Rick and I'd been apart since we'd left the United States.

While I waited for Rick to return, I put a pot of potato soup with leeks on the camp stove but forgot to pay attention to the flame and it boiled dry. I looked across the field at how far I needed to go for water. Too far. I poured the last of my scotch in the soup.

CHRISTIE AND I shared our stories. It was odd with the rally folks gone, the trampled grasses revealed a long view of the sea.

JUNE 26 At first light, we loaded up and I tucked low behind the tall windscreen to cut the cold. A highway sign had me smiling. "End crawler lane" was where the slow lane merged.

Stopped for coffee to warm up at Forres on the Moray coast just thirty miles east of Inverness. Getting off the bike, two elderly gents stepped very close and apparently had a story to share. It was a very, very long tale. When they walked away, arm in arm, Christie and I looked at each other. "Do you have any idea what that was about?" I asked her.

"I didn't understand a single word," she said and I had to agree.

We found an optometrist's office to get the screw replaced on Christie's glasses and mine adjusted. The helmets had continued to wreak havoc on them.

HE WAS A veiny-faced man with strikingly protuberant ears that trembled with every movement of his head. "No charge," he said shaking those ears. "Jes' Scottish hospitality."

Castles, quaint towns and green countryside flew by until we happened on a series of metal buildings that looked like blimp hangars. "Chivas Regal" was painted on the sides in letters two stories high. Rick slowed down. Heavy fences with razor wire discouraged break-ins.

DRIVING BY A warehouse full of Chivas I couldn't sample and golf courses I couldn't play was torture. Didn't exit at Carnoustie but drove over a toll bridge to arrive at the real home of golf, St. Andrews.

Booked lodging and packed our gear up three flights to a tiny room. The bathroom was down two flights, a hazard of not wanting to spend much money. But I didn't come to spend time in the room, I was eager to walk the hallowed grounds of St. Andrews.

It was late in the day but the sun wouldn't set until almost midnight so we had time. The course was just a few blocks away.

"There it is," I said, pointing. I knew my voice was choked with emotion. The oldest golf course in the world. "The holiest of holies," I whispered.

We started our walk on number 17, the road hole with the notorious bunker.

ON CERTAIN DAYS, St. Andrews is closed to golfers and open as a public park. We were in luck and free to walk the course.

I looked down into a trap so deep it had stairs for access and asked Rick, "So if martyrs were torched for their beliefs in the 1500s, are these traps today's version of torture?" But no one answered. Rick was too engrossed in the fact that his feet had met the turf at the Royal & Ancient to hear me.

JUNE 27 It flew in the face of everything that's holy to think about playing such a great course without real golf gear but I couldn't help myself. I asked the starter what it might take.

"We normally use a lottery system for tee times," he said. "But," and my pulse raced with anticipation, "the British Open is set to play here and we're closin' the links to prepare. You can play tomorrow with proof of suitable handicaps," he finished.

No problem! Both of our handicaps were low enough. I was ecstatic until I remembered that we didn't have handicap cards with us. Christie tried to concoct a cut-and-paste model but without a printer, scissors, or tape she couldn't make it happen.

We wandered the town to see the castle, monastery and University. Age and experience had crumbled the walls of the castle and tiny pink and white flowers grew in the cracks. The University is the third oldest in Britain, behind Oxford and Cambridge. I felt smarter just being there.

I was glad we were walking because when I was sitting, my hip still throbbed from getting dumped in Ayr. The mirror in our room showed a cauliflower-shaped cluster of purple bruises sprouting on my left hip. They'd flowered into a blend of yellow and blue that would have been pretty on canvas but not on my butt.

I sensed that Rick was mentally adjusting our itinerary. "Are you tempted to stick around for the Open?" I asked.

"Well. They're hiring. Or we could volunteer," he was pensive.

"It's okay with me. It might even be fun to be part of the action," I said. "As long as I don't get stuck working in a parking lot."

"Good point. It's possible we wouldn't see any golf," Rick's tone turned somber. "But we'd see more if we're here than if we're miles away," he finished.

"Got any lodging ideas?" I asked. We'd already checked hotels, inns, and campgrounds for the coming weeks and had gotten that "you must be kidding" look.

"Hmmm. Let's stick with Plan A," he said.

"I think we must be further down the alphabet than that," I said and we laughed in unison.

I stopped for another haircut. Chatting with the friendly barber, I shared my conflicting views of staying for the Open. He offered that we could lay our bed rolls out in his barber shop and gave us the number of a friend who could probably get us tournament jobs. It was a generous offer and removed the obstacles.

Later, exploring the golf museum, we again reviewed our options. With more time to think about it, Christie said, "It's kinda hard to want to hang out in England for an extra couple of weeks waiting for the Open when all of Europe is waiting for us."

I had to agree, but promised myself a return to St Andrews before Saint Peter called me home. On our way out of town, we swung by the barber shop to decline his kind offer.

In Stirling, we stopped at the Wallace Monument. An audio commentary described the campaign for freedom and victory at The Battle of Stirling Bridge in 1297. The Wallace sword and mementos of the character played by Mel Gibson in *Braveheart* were on display. I'm nearly six feet tall and the sword towered above me. It was wider than me, too. I had my doubts that even Mel could have wielded the monster.

FROM THE TOP of the tower, the view was breathtaking. Directional arrows pointed to the Trossachs in the west, the city of Stirling and the Ochil and Pentland hills to the east. Climbing back down, my mind was centuries behind.

The story of Wallace's trial made me wish I'd been a history teacher. It would be so easy to bring these dramatic events to life, I thought. Yet none ever did for me. All this was new. Had I slept my way through school?

THE CAMPGROUND IN Edinburgh was set in a pasture, with an on-site pub. The buildings had once been the estate's stable. A cluster of locals gathered at the pub and bought us drinks. They chatted up politics, American presidents, British faults, and how wonderful life was in Scotland. They knew a bit about Scotch whiskey, too, so we sampled and they kept buying.

Our camp neighbors, Heinz and Asrid, from Germany, were on a month-long trip on a small dirt bike with homemade saddlebags. Lots of ways to travel if you want the experience but feel the pinch of a budget.

JUNE 28 At 6:00 a.m. it was pouring but I needed to use the bathroom. I pulled my light velour jacket from the stuff sack I used as a pillow and crawled around the tent collecting my shower gear. A zip-lock bag of lotions, coins, hair brush, shampoo, soap, and chamois towel. I sloshed off to the shower room. Fussing with the knobs, I wondered, will the water turn on? It did. Will it be warm? Not very. Every shower operated with its own rules and we hadn't seen the worst of them, yet.

CAUGHT THE BUS into Edinburgh. Walked on slippery cobblestones through the mist and big crowds to Holyrood Palace at the opposite end of the Royal Mile from Edinburgh Castle. The Palace has served as a residence of the royal family since the 15th century. The brochure said that Queen Elizabeth II spends one week a year there "but otherwise the palace is open to the public." I failed to see "but." What are the odds? Apparently, really good. She was there. We left.

Walking back up the mile, I noticed that shops selling kilts weren't just for tourists. These guys really wore the plaid skirts and tasseled knee highs when we might wear tuxedos. I liked the outfits and considered getting kitted out myself. The prices were quite dear, though, so I passed on the opportunity to dress like a Scottish gentleman.

At an internet café, we checked our credit card statements and cleared 24 messages. Needed to mail checks to American Express and MasterCard. It was fairly easy because we carried

U.S. postage and envelopes. The system was that when we had outgoing mail, Christie approached a stranger who looked American, asked when they were going home and if it was in the next few days, asked them to drop an envelope or two in a mailbox on the other side of the pond. We only got one rejection during the whole trip.

JUNE 29 Had a camp breakfast of yogurt, biscuits, and instant coffee at a table with fellow campers about the ages of our daughters. Packed up and hit the road at 10:00 a.m., which seemed to be about the time we usually got going.

A WHITE DISC of sun bravely pushed its way through the grey landscape. It was just the two of us at Hadrian's Wall. Not another living soul as far as we could see. Was that chariots and hoofbeats I heard? Activity from twenty centuries ago?

Rick went exploring and I sat in the grass with my journal.

"Life is bigger with so much history. My country carries the mantle of 'most powerful in the world' but we're a young country. Here, I'm bombarded by a rich and long past. Deep roots. It's disquieting that as a citizen of the world's leader, I had to leave in order to understand that."

I WALKED ALONG the wall, built by the Romans in AD 122 as a defensive fortification. They couldn't defeat the Scots, so they fenced them out. I walked by a sign indicating that troops had lived here in AD 137.

THE WALLED CITY of York is a medieval town nestled in the valley. We found a guest house near the wall and walked to town for an "early bird" dinner, which in British life meant before 8:00 p.m.

After dinner, we chanced on a ghost-walking-tour. The guide led us along the river, to a tower where Jews committed suicide and up Shambles Street, once famous for its butcher shops but now simply for being narrow. The story goes that a love-struck couple from feuding families carried on their love affair from their respective balconies. I looked up. Sure enough, if they were young and flexible, it was possible to kiss across the street.

Our home-stay hosts were an unfriendly duo. We determined that they must have gone into the hospitality business for the income and their good location made it possible, but they had no interest in us or our well-being. We slept on rough bunk beds in a room crowded with books, old shoes, and bric-a-brac.

JUNE 30   After a bite of breakfast, we went in search of another guidebook recommendation from Rick Steves. This time it was the Jorvik underground village, purported to be "the best preserved Viking city ever excavated."

WE PAID THE fee. Feeling like we might be succumbing to a tourist rip-off, we climbed into a small cart. The first surprise was when the trolley spun around and we rode backward through time. The deeper underground we went the further back the calendar rolled.

We rode past chunks of buildings, piles of charred wood and broken pottery, arriving in the Viking settlement of Jorvik. It was AD 975. We heard the voices of gossiping neighbors, smelled the smoke of cooking and the stench of trash. The cart turned around and we moved slowly forward, climbing back to street level and modern day York. The ride through a thousand years of history had Disney overtones but clambering out of the cart, I felt much better educated about the past and the importance of digging it up.

AT THE AMERICAN Express office we booked overnight ferry passage from Hull to Rotterdam. I gave our stamped bills to a couple from Florida and they said they'd be happy to mail them.

Less than an hour out of York, we rode onto the ferry and lashed the bike in the motorcycle section with the help of the on-board stewards. The bunks were narrow. No sink in the room. Bathroom down the hall. But mainland Europe in the morning!

OUR ON-BOARD ROOM was the size of a phone booth but it was ours for the night. We locked our gear in the room and headed for the dining area. Sandwiches and Dutch beer, some new friends and their wine, card games, and we headed to bed.

"Don't tell me how educated you are, tell me how much you have traveled."

– MOHAMMED

CHAPTER 7

THE CONTINENT

JULY 1   A blaring loudspeaker nearly knocked us out of bed, announcing our arrival in Rotterdam within the hour. It was 5:30 a.m. British time and we'd partied like fools the night before.

I stumbled to the bathroom and splashed water in all the necessary places. Menopause was just refusing to happen. Back at home I might be glad but on a long motorcycle trip I would have welcomed the absence of periods. I added that to a list of things I couldn't control.

WE AROSE WITHOUT shining. Two cups of excellent but expensive coffee and some dry raisin rolls and we rode off the ferry into Holland. Good-bye English language. Hello right side of the road.

Riding at 75 mph I noticed that the exit numbers were increasing instead of decreasing which probably meant we were going the wrong way. Christie's niece was competing in an international swim meet in the village of Vught, near 's-Hertogenbosch, and we were headed there. A quick gas stop confirmed that we needed to reverse direction.

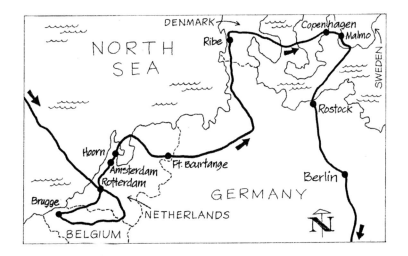

Found a room at the Terminus Inn. It was up a steep flight of stairs behind the bar. It was noisy and smoky but convenient for getting a beer before bed or an extra glass for water. Breakfast service began when the bar closed.

While Christie moved our gear into the room, I went in search of a place to park. On my third trip around the block, I realized that, at least in this town, parking for bicycles was labeled, "Cycle Parkeren." For a motorbike it was, "Bike parkeren." It was easy once I got the vocabulary figured out.

I PLANNED TO leave a few messages for my niece and with luck have a meal together. I took a leisurely shower and shampoo. Caught up on my writing. Worked on my finger-nails, wondering if they'd ever look female again. Two hours later, Rick was still sound asleep. I wrote in my journal. *"This adventure is more exhausting than he realizes. He drops off every time his feet and head are even close to level."*

JULY 2   The cold platters in the dining room were clear evidence that our tasty English, Irish, and Scottish breakfasts were over. From now on it would be dense bread and rolls with the heft of the ones Heidi tucked in her knapsack. Platters of room-temperature cheese and cold cuts and an occasional hard-boiled egg completed a "continental" breakfast. Why did that surprise me? It made sense that a "continental breakfast" is what they serve on "the continent." The good part was that I could make a picnic lunch by bundling a bit of the breakfast buffet in a headscarf.

We walked to a bicycle rental kiosk and immediately had a communication problem. Dutch is difficult and, contrary to popular travel lore, English is not spoken everywhere. I wasn't sure how we were going to communicate until I realized that the man was a Dutch Mexican. We spoke Spanish and we got along famously.

We rode past Camp Vught, one of just two SS concentration camps outside Nazi Germany. Here, 31,000 Jews, resistance fighters, hostages, gypsies, homosexuals, black marketers, and criminals had been imprisoned. There wasn't anything to see except wire fencing and a formidable building but it was a reminder that Europeans live with the evidence of WWII in their backyards.

BICYCLE RIDING IS a national pastime in this flat, populated country, so, we weren't surprised but amused to learn that it's customary for the Dutch to own a few. One is for riding to work, on Sunday rides and where there's safe parking. The other is a "beer bike," for riding to the tavern. We'd seen them but hadn't appreciated their place on the transportation ladder. They were uniformly rusty and cost about the same as a six-pack. When your "beer bike" got nicked, stolen, we were told, you nick the next one. The last guy out of the bar took a taxi.

THE LEAVES DRIPPED with lightly shed rain but the ground was dry on the ten-foot-wide pathway over the dike. We stopped for dinner and there wasn't a single word on the menu that resembled a food choice in my vocabulary. We both took French in high school and knew a fair amount of Spanish from our years sailing the Mexican coast. But I knew absolutely no Dutch except a plausible version of "Thank you." We ordered by pointing at plates on nearby tables.

We never did hook-up with my niece but the stop had been restful and I was fully recovered from the bruisings of tipping over. We mounted up for the ride through Ghent to Brugge (Bruges), Belgium.

Rick had to keep his eyes on the road but I watched the side roads, amazed at the sheer numbers of bicycles. A short woman carrying a long dry cleaning bag high enough to keep the plastic bag out of the spokes. Men with briefcases. Older men on old bicycles. Children straddling the handlebars while Mom balanced groceries and lots of ladies riding with bundles balanced on their heads.

In the distance I saw what looked like a boat in the middle of a field of sunflowers. I blinked. Twice. A mirage? A sailboat stranded in a field of flowers? A few minutes later my sanity was restored: the boat was tacking back and forth in a very narrow canal but the ground was so flat it wasn't visible. Holland. Bikes and dikes.

NEAR BRUGGE, CHRISTIE saw caravans parked off to our right so I circled back to St. Michael's Camping Ground. On-site were clay tennis courts, a restaurant and bar, and box hedges between campers.

We walked into town and had a deli lunch, using a church wall as a picnic table. Our path crisscrossed canals and we passed buildings with medieval history. At a grocery store, I filled my pack with provisions. A bottle of wine and a frozen entree of seafood pasta for dinner. Plus a kiwi and some blackberries. We bought a few packs of Kleenex, too, because the camp bathrooms didn't even have dispensers. Never mind being empty, they didn't intend to ever provide paper goods.

BACK IN CAMP, I spied a treasure sticking out of an overgrown hedge. It was a table leg. I tugged and came up with a prize. A small round metal table had been discarded. I lugged it home where Rick scrubbed it off and ingeniously folded our tent bag to even the legs. Having our camp stove waist high instead of on the ground was a luxury to be celebrated. We dragged two plastic chairs from the pub's courtyard and I heated the frozen dinner entree while Rick opened the wine. We toasted the table and chairs. And travel. And each other.

At the pub we watched France trounce Italy on the telly. It was a raucous crowd. Following the game, the campground was noisy with celebrants but I slept the sleep of angels, dreaming of tables and chairs.

JULY 3 Crawled out of the tent to start the coffee and saw that our pilfered table and chairs had been pilfered. Christie grumbled her way to the shower.

Stretching from my crouched position over the stove on the ground, I was shocked at the sight of our table and chairs being held aloft by three adults headed my way. One held the table overhead and the other two carried the chairs. I wondered if they spoke English and considered pelting them with a hard roll.

Turned out they were from South Africa. Some of the most charming folks we met. Apparently, partying English soccer fans had played a late night prank re-arranging everything moveable in the campground. We shared coffee as well as the chairs and had a good laugh over the mess while chatting about travel, politics, lifestyles, and parenting. They invited us to stay at their home in South Africa someday.

WE PUT ON our tourist hats and bought tickets for a canal ride. The guide spoke alternately in French, Dutch, and English. Forty-three bridges, some 500 years old. Twenty-one churches and only 20,000 people.

Climbed the bell tower and watched the machinery of gears whir and clank. The bells clanged. Holding hands, we gazed down at the red tiled roofs of Brugge, Belgium.

AT THE HUISBROUWERIJ Straffe brewery we toasted Belgium with a frosty beer. At the church of Our Lady we gazed at a Michelangelo statue of Madonna and child, crypts, and tombs to the tune of mournful music. Shops were repetitions of each other, all peddling lace and chocolate, chocolate and lace.

The Basilica of Heilig Bloed is the church that owns a vial of Christ's blood. I was on a mission to find it and we did, in a medieval chapel next to a gothic church with an ornate chalice. It wasn't impressive but I'd put it on my "must see" list because I'd read that it was taken to Brugge in AD 150, after the Second Crusade. Okay, box checked.

I ATE BELGIAN waffles, not because I love waffles but because it seemed like something one did in Belgium. We rode rented bicycles along a ring road that ran next to a canal and under four windmills. Traffic surged in waves. Old men balanced plastic buckets on their handlebars, women in skirts with shiny black patent shoes pedaled with amazing ease. An agile young mother somehow carried three children and bags of groceries. It was peaceful, pottering among them, caught in the gentle flow of a town going about its business. On bicycles!

JULY 4   Middle-aged American women don't typically get excited about a tour of Europe that includes crawling out of a tent, firing up a four-inch propane stove, and heading for the public showers. But for me, it was heaven.

HEAVEN WAS 350 kinds of Belgian beer. The darkest, "Trappist," was a close second to Guinness. Hated to leave all those choices but we pushed on toward Amsterdam.

AT A SIDEWALK lunch in Utrecht, Rick's hamburger wasn't expensive but an order of fries doubled the cost. Easy to skip; our leathers didn't have elastic waistbands. A motorcycle camping trip sounds energetic but in reality it was quite sedentary. We sat on the bike, strolled through towns, ate and slept.

Nearing Amsterdam, we didn't see any signs directing us to camping so we followed the signs to Tourist Information. In a parking lot with thousands of bicycles, we lost the trail and rode on. Out of the maze of strange signs Rick spotted a welcome "Camping Zeeburg." Arrows directed us straight into a sea of tents.

I showed our European camping card to the office and they kept it, which we'd gotten used to. We would get it back when we paid at check out. In Britain, the camp card wasn't recognized and we'd had to give them our passports. I preferred handing over the laminated green camp card.

WHILE CHRISTIE SIGNED us in, I looked around. An army of young people lay half in, half out of their tents. Vending machines dispensed Heineken and condoms.

"Could be really noisy tonight," I mumbled with the tent pegs between my teeth.

"Why?" Christie asked.

I didn't answer. She'd figure it out.

We locked our valuables on the bike, snapped on the nylon cover and took the tram into the city.

A network of bike paths had stop lights, turn signals and sign posted right-of-way rules. Folks sported multicolored hairstyles and every conceivable clothing style from funky to high fashion. Cars were so small you could ride them indoors.

We asked questions and learned that "bars" sold liquor, "cafés" peddled food and "coffee shops" served marijuana and mushrooms.

IN OUR FIRST coffee shop, we understood the menu about as well as a five-year-old comprehends a Russian opera. Rick ordered a Thai joint with a filter tip. We aren't pot smokers but unlike our former President, we did inhale.

Emboldened by a few puffs between bouts of coughing, we headed for the infamous red light district. According to Rick, this was "Good stuff, part two."

SCANTILY CLAD WOMEN stood in storefront windows, using their bodies to lure customers. They were thin, fat, ugly or lovely; a style for every customer. Their tactics were as aggressive as a time share salesman on the *malecon* in Puerto Vallarta. The only difference was that instead of waving brochures, they gyrated their hips.

Apparently, I stayed in front of one window too long and missed something that Christie told me about. A gal wearing only hot pink lace panties motioned for her to enter the cubicle. Christie said she did a reciprocating wiggle-waggle but joined me around the corner instead. A guy's greatest fantasy might have unfolded. Opportunity lost.

Back home in the tent we had great sex with the tent flap open. It seemed appropriate with risqué Amsterdam just across the water.

JULY 5   After coffee and rolls at the campground pub, we went back to town. Today would be museums, a culture day. But wasn't last night "cultural" Amsterdam, too? Being me, we had to talk about it.

Seated at the tram stop, Rick said, "You look deep in thought, anything specific?"

I smiled at him, wiping rain drops from my glasses. Tucking them inside my pocket, I said, "I'm wrestling with the concept that today's plan is to visit museums. I wrote in my journal that today was a 'culture day.' But I think last night was more about Amsterdam culture than museums will be. So which is it? Isn't grocery shopping or watching kids play in a park as valid a travel experience as the ones we need to buy tickets for?"

"I vote for both," Rick said as the tram pulled up, sparing him from a longer answer.

The entry to Anne Frank's house was through Otto's office. Quotes from her diary were on the walls. She was thirteen when she wrote, "The sun is shining, the sky is deep blue, there's a magnificent breeze and I'm longing – really longing – for everything: conversation, freedom, friends."

"How lucky we are," I thought, vowing never to take my freedom for granted. And to not complain. My struggles were so trivial.

The Secret Annex was preserved as the Hiding Place that it was. Anne's story was a testimonial to the goodness in most but layered with the horror of self-centered righteousness turned to fascism. Quotes were on display from Orwell, Einstein and de Gaulle, disdaining the nationalism of labeling as "they" everything that doesn't belong to "us."

DEEP IN PENSIVE thought, we found a lunch café. I was having difficulty processing the proximity of the Red Light District to Anne Frank's house. The waitress thought we were Dutch, which I found to be a huge compliment. Seldom were we taken for Americans.

We strolled beside canals, houseboats, a flower market. Two bicycles sped by while the couple kissed. Hard to imagine it was possible if I hadn't seen it with my own eyes. I reached for Christie's elbow and twirled her into my arms for a sidewalk kiss. She stumbled over my foot and the kiss landed in air. How on earth did they kiss on speeding bicycles? We couldn't even kiss while walking.

My favorite Impressionist artist is Vincent Van Gogh and Amsterdam was my chance to see two hundred paintings in chronological order. The self-portraits revealed his genius as well as his progressive madness. Leaning as close as the ropes allowed, I examined the landscapes and could almost hear the lyrics of "Starry, Starry Night."

After a couple of hours, we left the Impressionists and moved to Rembrandt in the next building. A bit dark after the vivid colors of Van Gogh.

There were times, like when it was raining, when we were lost, when I'd rather play golf than set up the tent, that I doubted our sanity. But I didn't think that in Amsterdam.

We went back to the red light district for a glimpse of modern art by day, taking us full circle with Christie's query earlier in the morning. I said, "About your 'culture' question, I really do think it's both. We find the past in museums and the present on the streets. Reality exists in the mix of the two. And we've got twelve more weeks to test that theory."

IT WAS BILLED as the "world's largest internet café" and with 650 stations how could I disagree? Lisa's email had her new phone number and I was intent on trying to call. Back at the campground, I headed for the pay phones and took my place at the end of a long line of teenagers. Kids calling parents. Parent calling kid.

JULY 6 Edam, like the cheese, was delightful. A nattily attired parking patrol lady instructed where we could park.

A GREY RIVER flowed like mercury under a bridge. Standing at its arc, the reflection formed a circle that was framed by a riot of crimson geraniums. I went back to the bike to dig the camera out of its pouch.

Flakes of croissant fell on my lap and I scooped them back into my napkin gently like flower petals. Rick asked, "Did you ever wonder why we call a half door, a 'Dutch door'?"

I looked in the direction he was pointing. The cars parked along the curb were bite-size but he was asking me to look at the shop doors. Their bottom halves were closed and tops open. Before I could answer, he had more Dutch queries for me.

"How about Dutch treat, where'd that come from?" he asked.

"I have no idea," I said, laughing. "Any other Dutch delights we need to research?"

"Well, I'm not much good in the galley but I know that small Swedish pancakes are Dutch babies," he said draining the last of a tiny cup of very black coffee.

IT WAS A short ride to Hoorn, founded in AD 716. It's less than 35 kilometers from Amsterdam and should be on every tourist's must-stop list. But if you go and see an American, take a picture. No one will believe you.

A small fleet of Dutch schooners headed out to sea and a group of sixtyish ladies was gathering for a ride. I asked what was the occasion for so many sailboats going out on a Thursday. "To sail" was the collective response. I liked that. Having fun was reason enough to have fun but my American self still instinctively expected an event, a schedule, rules and ribbons.

We rode a long dike to Hindeloopen, another Rick Steves favorite. We arrived with an onslaught of tourist buses so we hit the road.

I SCRIBBLED NOTES in my pocket journal while Rick drove. *"There's an ease about being amongst the Dutch. They seem to enjoy life and while the pace is brisk they aren't frantic. Life is about pleasure and work is a means to attain it, not a goal in itself."* Hmmm. I put the journal away.

We were headed for the Fort recommended by the couple we'd met at the Dublin campground. We stopped for a drawbridge that was letting a sailboat pass. In the distance, more sailboats looked as though they were sailing next to cows in the bread-crust-colored fields. The juxtaposition was cartoonish.

AT FORT BOURTANGE, we nicknamed our gruff proprietor "Brumhilda" but the cabin was a nice change from tent life and just $25 for the night. We dumped the bed rolls on the narrow bunks and locked the door behind us.

The Fort was shaped like a star and surrounded by a moat, complete with cannons and windmills. Built in 1593, it was obsolete by the time it was completed.

WE SAT ON the top of the fort's wall with our feet dangling over the 100-foot-deep moat. I tried to envision the cannon balls that were meant to be volleyed at approaching Germans nearly 500 years earlier. The happy little flowers sprouting through the cracks in the wall made a different statement.

A handful of tourists in small groups passed us. We made a game of trying to decide where they were from based on snatches of conversations and clothing styles.

A man with a camera on a tripod introduced himself. Hermann was taking photographs for commercially produced postcards. While he waited for the sun to deliver the effect he was after, he and Rick chatted. I listened vaguely and watched the blades of a windmill churn.

"How does it go, seeing Europe on a motorbike?" Hermann asked.

"Well. Good and bad. Do you really want to know?"

"Give it a go. I'm waiting for the light and love to learn."

"OK. Here's the honest truth. Things rarely work out as planned but they do work out for the best. The key is flexibility." Christie patted my leg and smiled in agreement.

"What are Americans like?" he asked next.

I took a little longer on that one but Hermann was good at waiting for the right light so I guessed he was a patient man.

"I'm afraid we're loud and we usually travel in groups. Before this trip, Christie and I lived in Mexico, on our sailboat, for four years. We noticed then that Americans tend to let doors slam. We slouch in our chairs and put our feet up. Americans carry a self-assuredness that makes us look like we own the place. It's not pretty."

My description seemed to depress us both into a silence which I broke after a few moments. "Tell me about Europeans."

Hermann smiled. "Well, the Swiss are on time and they love their rules. Italians are sharp dressers and they're most often late except for the *passeggiata*. As far as rules go, Italians will pocket your money and keep the change."

He inhaled deeply but I figured he wasn't through. "The French don't travel much outside France but they do enjoy their leisure, which is why Hitler walked over them so easily. Contrast that with the Germans, who leave Germany every chance they get. They'd rather be anyplace else. We Dutch want to chat it up and because our English is nearly flawless. You'll get to know my countrymen the best during your travels." He finished the long burst and looked quite pleased with his speech.

The sun was nearing the angle Hermann must have been looking for. He got busy and we left, waving our "goodbyes."

Our cabin was just 500 meters from the fort. This was our first night in a camping cabin but I hoped it wouldn't be our last. It was the best of both worlds, cheap like camping but indoors.

There was a bare light globe but no running water, a cook top stove and tea kettle but no dishes or pans. Two hundred yards away was a building with dishwashing sinks, laundry facilities, showers, a restaurant and bar. It was neat, clean, and quiet. Nirvana.

JULY 7 Rick spread our wrinkled map of Europe across the table and I moved my coffee cup to make room. I loved that we'd inserted ourselves into a world where we could decide the day's activities by looking at a map of Europe.

I voted for heading toward southern Germany because I guessed that the Scandinavian countries would be too expensive. And cold. Christie convinced me that since we were already this far north and might never return, we should see Denmark. With just two votes, it was always a tie when we disagreed. One of us had to give in and today it was me.

Brumhilda interrupted our itinerary musings. Her mass filled the doorway and her grim look didn't need translation. Clearly, we'd failed some sort of test. Using sign language, I tried to say we'd leave in about an hour. She folded her face into an expression of tolerance.

Supervising our check-out, she watched me sweep the floor while Christie wiped the stove top. Hands on hips, she stood like a drill sergeant until she deemed the cabin clean enough. She dismissed us with a gruff wave and a grunt. We rode away before she had a chance to find another job for us. Had to laugh.

Germany was going to be a tough pill to swallow after the ribald Brits, fun-loving Irish, ruddy-cheeked Scots, and thoroughly delightful Dutch.

"Whatever you do in life will be insignificant. But be sure to do it."

– GANDHI

CHAPTER 8

RODENTS AND RAIN

A TORRENT OF cars passed in a blur. Speeds of 120 to 150 mph were the norm. It was a sobering reminder to stay in the far right lane. Watch the rearview mirrors. And pray, if I had time.

CARS DODGED PAST and shot over the horizon. We were rodents on an airport runway. I peered over Rick's right shoulder, the needle pointed at 88. I tucked low behind him and mumbled a few passive prayers. Being a Presbyterian, I didn't have much biblical ammunition.

LEAVING THE GERMAN autobahn in Denmark, the concept of "speed" changed. The Danes leave no wiggle room between the posted limit and actual speed. One mile per hour over was grounds for a ticket. And they were reportedly very expensive. I didn't want to find out just how expensive.

Ribe is Denmark's oldest village, settled by Vikings in AD 700. A Danish biker on one of our ferry rides had said it was worth a visit, so here we were.

A room that included breakfast is a "veresler," so that's what Christie asked for. The term must have meant "huge room" because ours was. It was also up a flight of stairs that started behind the bar. I spread our gear out more than usual just because I could.

Back downstairs, I ordered a tall Tuborg beer and we shared a steaming platter of cabbage, gravy, and potatoes. Bikers shouldn't drink and drive and I never did. We either had wine at the camp site or a brew within walking distance.

A BROCHURE ON the table touted a "night watchman tour" that sounded intriguing. In the 1800s, the Night Watchman was in charge of maintaining order in the streets while watching for fires, floods, and mayhem. The job was taken over by the police in 1902 but re-introduced as a tourist attraction in 1932.

We added layers of clothing and headed to the starting place at 10:00 p.m. The streets were washed in the grey light of a single street lamp. I shivered in the fog. I'd forgotten the camera but rationalized that it might be good to rely on memory. I'd been wondering if the promise of prints had kept me from paying attention to details. Tonight I'd find out.

Our guide was the town mayor by day and spoke seven different languages during the tour. With a lantern in his right hand, cape flowing behind, and a large medallion around his neck, he chanted and sang his way across town, magically transforming the winding streets into a Halloween eve in AD 1200.

JULY 8 Breakfast was an unpleasant buffet of tired cheese and warm salami in a smoky back room off the bar. An intense longing for British fare overcame me. Soft eggs, toast in a silver rack, baked beans, warm tomatoes, and banger sausages served on pretty plates. I did the math and figured we had about 70 more mornings before British breakfasts would be offered. I sighed, shuddered, and put a hard roll, a slice of fatty salami and a hard-boiled egg on my plate.

WE CROSSED A toll bridge, heading for Copenhagen, København. Sailboats raced below. Denmark has 400 islands so these folks actually sailed their boats instead of leaving them for months on end in marina slips as is common in America.

We found a campground in a World War I fort on the waterfront, complete with cannons facing the sea. We were lucky to have arrived at Camping Fort Strand at 3:00. At 3:30 it was full.

Walking on the beach, we found ourselves in a nude bathing area. I tried, not very hard, to not stare at the amazing blonde on the yellow towel with the perfect legs and perky boobs. She seemed to be a natural blonde but I didn't notice because I was with Christie and know better.

Not to be left out, Christie made sure I knew what she'd seen: a man with a larger than normal appendage. I told her I was shocked that she even knew what sizes were possible other than yours truly. We chuckled over the accidental encounter and promised to check each other out to test our memories when we got back to the tent.

Caught a bus into the city, got off at the "centrum" and immediately discovered why the campground was full. It was the annual Jazz Festival, one of the largest music events in Europe.

The harbor was lively. Wearing bright-colored festival T-shirts, we moved with the masses, thoroughly enjoying the jazz. Street performers, artists and random other musicians filled the spaces between tourists. We bought a Chinese box dinner and dined, seated on the sidewalk with our feet in the street.

AT 6:00 P.M. the stores closed. With thousands of people crowding the sidewalks, it was surprising to our American profit-crazed sensibilities that the shop keepers weren't milking the opportunity to hear their cash registers ring.

The next surprise was that the Tivoli Gardens aren't gardens. It's a family-style carnival combined with New Orleans ambiance. Fast food, karaoke, fun rides, and ice cream stands were side by side with elegant restaurants, jazz, brandy and wine cafés. Folks were dressed in everything from date night finery to beach wear. What the crowd had in common was a happy attitude. We joined in their spirit but the thought crossed my mind that my mom would be horrified that I was mingling with the well-groomed wearing shower sandals, wrinkled shorts, and a T-shirt, even though it was new and clean.

WE TOOK THE bus back to the campground at 11:00 p.m. and got there just in time to enjoy a fireworks show right over our tent. When that show ended, we ducked inside for the fireworks prompted by our walk through the nude beach.

JULY 9 At 5:00 a.m. I was awake. I got up quietly, leaving Christie gently sawing logs and took off on foot in the direction of the oceanfront. Seated on a bench, I intended to simply soak in the stillness when a beautiful thing happened.

A young woman, perhaps 35, walked across the pier. A vision. She dropped her robe not 30 feet from me. Raising her arms over her head, she dove into the frigid water with barely a ripple.

I huddled deeper in my fleece, wondering how on earth she could swim in the icy water when I could barely sit on the bench. A few hundred yards offshore she circled back and completed her swim with long, strong, smooth strokes. She climbed out and toweled off. Without hurrying, she wrapped the robe around her slim body and walked back the way she'd come. That she was quite beautiful was part of my enjoyment but the freedom to be naked mattered, too.

WHEN I WOKE up, Rick was gone. A grey dawn crept over the rim of the sea but I didn't see any sign of hot coffee so I crawled back in my sleeping bag. When Rick returned, he told me about the magic of watching a lovely Dane perform a ritualistic nude swim in icy water. Like the Dutch, the Danes demonstrated an enviable comfort level.

After a camp breakfast, we sprang for tickets on an all-day bus loop tour. Our "guide" wasn't a person but a grainy recording. The stops didn't match the map and it didn't run very often, which made it more of a hop-off–good luck-hopping-back-on tour.

WE GOT OFF at Rosenborg Castle just outside of the city center and next to the National Gallery and Botanical Gardens. I got a kick out of the fact that the King had his quarters in the northern part of the castle and the Queen's chambers were in the southern end. Seemed to me that would preclude the need for divorce lawyers.

The statue of the little mermaid on a rock in the bay looked exactly like the postcard image and it was unimpressive. It was crafted by a little known sculptor, unveiled in 1913, and symbolizes a fairy tale by the Danish author and poet Hans Christian Andersen. Christie told me that it's the story of a young mermaid who fell in love with a prince who lived on land, and often came up to the edge of the water to look for her love. No wonder it wasn't on my radar. But 75% of all tourists visiting Copenhagen go to see it. Kind of validates the sheep-over-the-cliff theory.

In the Royal Copenhagen china shop we priced fancy breakables like children of nervous parents – with our hands clasped behind our backs. There was definitely some "wow" factor in a

$4,000 breakable coffee pot but I wasn't tempted to reach for my credit card.

We went to a movie theatre showing twenty-four films, all in English with Danish subtitles. Assigned seats, all-you-can-eat pizza, and a full liquor bar completed my list of surprises.

JULY 10 Leaving Denmark, we bought a small sticker for the saddle bags and all the groceries we could bungee to the saddle bags. Sweden would be expensive. The Øresund Bridge is the longest road and rail bridge in Europe, connecting Denmark with Malmö, Sweden. Wind gusts knocked us around and I was relieved to arrive safely on the other side. Christie said the views were stunning.

We followed the coastline from Trelleborg to Ystad. We'd been told that there were interesting fishing villages in the area and we were in search of one where we could stay for a few days, exploring on foot and waiting for sunshine.

ATE OPEN-FACE FRIED herring and onion sandwiches on paper plates and talked with a couple from Florida who were selling their sailboat to buy one in Sweden. Michael said, "They want 25% import duty and our boat's too big for the marina, anyway." He wore a wool fisherman knit sweater that couldn't have been part of his Florida wardrobe.

The weather was nasty. "Sailors in this part of the world are hardy souls," I said to Rick as we got back on the bike.

I WASN'T FEELING that hardy. I needed warm, dry weather, sooner rather than later. Over lunch, we had voted unanimously to explore Sweden some other decade and to divert immediately for the ferry to Germany.

RAIN PUMMELED OUR helmets and trickled down our necks. At the ferry dock, a sign indicated one was leaving for Rostock, Germany. We'd never heard of it but I figured we'd have the whole ferry ride to read up. By the time we found the correct loading queue we were too late. It was the fast ferry, a three-hour trip, and it left without us.

The next boat, the slow one, would leave in about 90 minutes and we were supposed to queue up in lane ten. I held my dripping glove in front of the ticket seller to indicate we'd rather wait indoors, if possible. She pointed to the terminal. We went inside but it was strangely deserted which gave us a feeling that something wasn't right. But at least there was a roof over our heads.

WE WAITED, WATCHING the bike being pelted by rain. When the cars started moving, we grabbed our helmets, stuffed them over wet hair, and ran outside. By the time we mounted up, the line of cars had vanished and the tarmac was empty.

I accelerated up the closest ramp but immediately knew it was the wrong ferry. The ramp was too steep, which I hadn't noticed in my haste and through a rain-spotted face mask. The angle was bad. Christie grabbed at my leather jacket. I could feel her tugging at the fabric while we bumped dangerously over metal grates and parallel to a rider's worst fear: narrow tracks. The rear tire caught in a track and over we went. We fell to the right and were pinned under the bike. Christie wriggled out and lifted the bike the couple of inches I needed to free my boot. Together, we managed to right it.

A guy in uniform at the top of the ramp stared at us as though we were misplaced wildlife. Christie shouted something about it being the wrong ferry, which I clearly recognized.

Back in the central ferry loading area, we were about as cheerful as two cats in a swimming pool. A car with an official seal on the door drove by at a parade pace but didn't respond to our waving arms and shouted questions. Another unhelpful Scandlines official casually waved us in the direction of a row of semi-trucks. No one but Christie could hear my wrath but my face mask was steaming.

At the foot of the ramp, sure enough, there was a short moveable sign that read, "Rostock." Relieved, soggy and pissed, we rode onto the ferry, split the lanes between semi-trucks, and parked in the bow.

A German biker helped us with the straps to secure the bike and we headed upstairs. Christie was slightly injured in the tip-over and I had every intention of being extra sensitive and helpful.

WE TOOK OVER a large table, spreading out enough wet gear to resemble a drying room at a laundromat. It had been a long odd day, from the windy ride across the bridge between Denmark and Sweden to the mishap on the cargo ferry. I was limping and sure my hip was bruised but Rick looked beat. I reminded myself to be gentle; he looked bruised in spirit.

I loaded a tray with comfort food and hot coffee, to which I would add a splash of the brandy I'd stowed in my pocket. Rain ran down the windows with such force it looked like they were power washing the boat.

SIX HOURS LATER we arrived in Rostock, a former German U-boat port. Christie had read a poster about there being a spa town nearby. Leaving the ferry, we went in search of Heiligendamm. Before we even got through Rostock, Christie tapped my shoulder and pointed at a brightly painted "Hotel" sign. I stopped. Sometimes the travel gods took care of us when we needed them most.

And more good luck: an English-speaking woman was in the lobby. It didn't take long to realize that only German and Russian were spoken. This piece of real estate had been behind the Iron Curtain and change was slow.

WE HAD A kitchen, balcony, TV, plush bedding, colorful comforters, and a giant bathtub. I created my own spa, soaking in bubbles. The cold, aches, and angst, mental and physical, washed away.

JULY 11   In blissfully warm sunshine, we walked to Heiligendamm wearing just shorts and sandals. It was reputedly the destination of royals in the 18th and early 19th centuries. Now, in the early 21st century, it was nearly vacant and deteriorating. German and Russian tourists played on the beach, ate in restaurants, rode bicycles, and seemed oblivious to the sinister towers dotting the beach front.

THE GUARD TOWERS were German lookouts, built for the purpose of keeping the locals from leaving. Empty machine gun ports that had been manned during my lifetime were stark reminders of what these people had endured.

We shopped for groceries and not a single product looked familiar. We were the other oddity in the market. Had an American ever shopped here before? We felt a heavy responsibility that we might be the only Americans some of these folks would ever see. We smiled a lot and spoke quietly.

DUE TO ROSTOCK'S location in a former Eastern Bloc country, everything was incredibly cheap. But, true to that stereotype, most of the shopkeepers looked miserable, as if they'd all recently had a root canal and expected another within the hour.

JULY 12   We needed new tires, a 12,000-mile check-up and the front fender fixed. I figured that Berlin, where the bike was built, was a reasonable place to get the work done. I stopped for directions at Tourist Information and Christie went in.

I WAITED PATIENTLY, hoping I was in the right line. *"Vo es BMW dealership, bitte?"* I spoke slowly. The only German I knew was "where is, please and thank you." It hadn't occurred to me that the English alphabet letters, BMW, wouldn't translate into what we were looking for. What on earth did they call the company? I pointed to the motorcycle outside and pantomimed the use of a wrench, I hoped she'd get that I meant "repair." She opened a map and pointed with a pretty polished nail. I circled the general area with a wet golf pencil and paid for the map.

WE RODE PAST the massive Brandenburg Gate just as Napoleon did in 1806 but I was feeling more overwhelmed than victorious. Christie held the map against the back of my leather jacket and called out street names that changed every few blocks from something "strasse" to something else "strasse." The city has a population of 3.5 million and it looked as though they each had a street named after them. It would have been funny if I hadn't been tired and frustrated. Train tracks ran parallel so I was focused.

By accident, we found a BMW dealership and pulled into the service bay. They couldn't work on the bike for three weeks but the manager pleasantly gave us some BMW stickers and called a different dealership. Off we went with our damp map.

We located the store and were greeted by Tobias Zimmerman, an English-speaking service manager extraordinaire. He said that we were the first Americans to return an exported bike to the factory for service.

Tobias said the work would be done in three days and found us a bargain room. He loaned us a dark grey 1200LT and we transferred our clothes, left the camping gear, and took off. The LT was

well-equipped with a radio, built-in solid saddle bags, and heated seats and grips. A smooth ride but not as nimble as the GS.

WE WENT IN search of our apartment, somewhere in East Berlin. Rick stopped next to the curb in front of a six-story building that matched the address on the scrap of paper in my hand. I got off and went up a half dozen concrete steps. I stared at a row of buttons with unrecognizable names next to them.

Turning to Rick, I shrugged, "What now?"

He got off and joined me. We looked up and down the street. Grey. Everything was the color of old iron. Including the shiny BMW we'd been loaned. The Iron Curtain had lifted but it could have been within the last hour.

A voice caught our attention and I looked up to see a woman hanging out of a third-floor window, waving her arms like a sprinkler gone awry. Either we were about to step on a land mine or she was our landlord. The door buzzed like a dentist drill and Rick yanked it open.

We climbed the steep stairs and met Lotte. She was talking but we had no idea what she was saying. I held up a pocket-size English-German dictionary and the tiny woman broke into a large grin that exposed more gaps than teeth and deepened the pleats around her mouth. She took possession of my dictionary and I never saw it again.

She lived in the back of what was once a single apartment and we had the front two-thirds. At the entry, she stepped past us and flipped a latch behind an enormous mirror. It swung open, revealing our bathroom. An image of Anne Frank's secret hideout came to mind.

With a quick punch to the mattress to be sure we'd be able to sleep and a double check that there were towels in the bathroom, we went back down to board the luxurious BMW loaner.

I PARKED IN front of a Berlin church and we wandered in. It was ornate and grand but had no aura of tranquility. It was noisy and the only church we visited in all of Europe that charged admission. It was only $4 but the others had requested donations. To us, there was a big difference between asking and demanding.

Our glasses needed repair again and I saw an optometrist sign across the street. We easily got them fixed but without the friendliness of the shop in Scotland.

Late in the afternoon, we had a picnic and explored Schloss Charlottenburg, the summer house for the Queen of Prussia in 1705. It's a half-mile long, which I was thinking would make for a long trek to the kitchen. We hadn't heard any English spoken since the BMW service manager but we'd seen lots of cigarette smoke.

It seemed every tourist was puffing away, intent on shortening their lives and polluting our picnics. We made it a quick stop.

JULY 13   For more than forty years, Checkpoint Charlie was a symbol of the Cold War. We stood in stunned silence, watching the human saga of separation scroll by on a screen in front of us. People got out by hiding under the floor boards of cars or shimmying across phone lines. One woman left on a day pass with her four-year-old in a shopping bag.

THE CREATIVE WAYS desperate people devised to sneak across the border and the courage to do so were thought-provoking. These people wanted what we take for granted: the ability to move freely and to live without fear.

THE EAST GERMAN checkpoint, Gestapo headquarters, and places Hitler lived and made his decisions all made my skin crawl. The war ended before I was born but the pain and suffering caused by so much hatred vibrated through the thick soles of my boots.

It occurred to me that if Ireland, Belgium, and Denmark had the aura of a woman aging gracefully, Berlin was a botched facelift. New construction looked like scars that wouldn't heal. Maybe I was having a mid-life crisis myself but my irritability even included the nature of the language. Its guttural growl sounded like an old man trying to expel a wad of phlegm.

JULY 14   Rode to Potsdam in light rain. The parks and palaces of Sanssouci were mind boggling due to size alone. The buildings were the residences of Prussian kings and German emperors but you had to buy tickets for each building at a single ticket office.

It was really set-up for bus tour groups because we had no way to know which buildings to see and which were closed. I gave up trying to figure it out in favor of enjoying the grounds. It was enough to imagine old Frederick the Great right here, enjoying life "without care," "sans souci."

The 1945 Potsdam Conference was a meeting of the Allies at the end of World War II, held at Cecilienhof. I saluted as we went by.

Another interesting ride-by was Babelsberg, the oldest large-scale film studio in the world. Since the fall of the Berlin Wall, it's been a major center of European film production. We closed out our Potsdam morning with a walk along the river Havel before returning to Berlin.

JULY 15 We got lost finding the dealership, sorted ourselves out and found it by luck. The bike was ready; washed and waxed with new tires. A new snout sat over the front tire where it belonged. She was "Woody" again.

I TOSSED THE old snout in the trash. It was foolish to have thought it could be re-attached, but it had served as a visual reminder not to be stupid.

We waved and hollered our thanks, "Bitte sehr." I found the way out of town but any direction would do as far as I was concerned. The BMW service had been impeccable but I wanted to escape Berlin. History said that wasn't a new thought.

We had dinner at a gas stop because we were hungry but that meant no wine or beer.

EVEN AT A gas station, food was served on real plates. No plastic. No paper cups or skimpy napkins. How civilized.

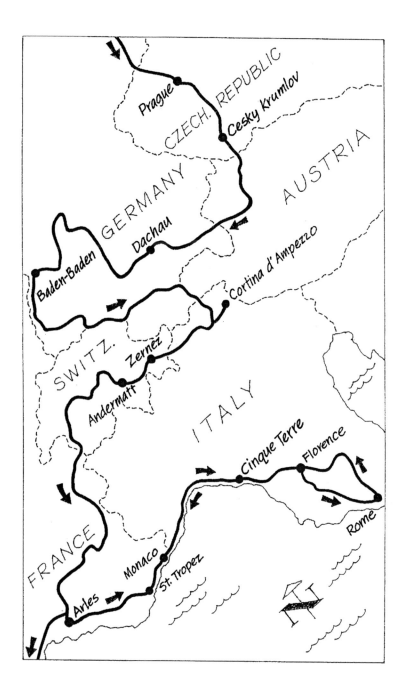

"For my part, I travel not to go anywhere, but to go. I travel for travel's sake. The great affair is to move."

– ROBERT LOUIS STEVENSON

CHAPTER 9

DETOUR

I DIDN'T KNOW what town we were in but when Christie went in to ask if the quaint, immaculate hotel had a room, I was pleased that the price was reasonable and included breakfast. A brisk walk and my autobahn tension receded.

CHURCH BELLS CHIMED every fifteen minutes, making our evening stroll a delight. English was spoken by a few shopkeepers so I learned some things. Unemployment was 20–50% but there wasn't an outpouring of frustration because "it hasn't been that long since the Iron Curtain fell." Seemed like a long time to us but European life goes back a thousand years so I guessed their idea of "time" had a bigger canvas.

JULY 16   After a good night's sleep, we left the village on the outskirts of Dresden and headed for Prague, Praha. There weren't any signs to guide us out of Germany and I thought about the towers and walls that discouraged leaving for so many years. There were plenty of signs directing

us to *"Umleitung"* though. We didn't want to go there so we ignored them. Only later did we find out that *umleitung* meant "detour." Literally, it means "redirect" but we didn't.

STOPPED FOR DIRECTIONS. The language the man spoke sounded more Italian than German but it really didn't matter because I didn't understand either. Without helpful words, I watched the path of his thick forefinger trace the ridge of a smudged map. I made a note of the first few road names and we roared off, waving our thanks.

If being lost means not having the slightest idea where you are, we were still lost. I stopped again. Two guys dressed in camogear, riding a Russian motorcycle with a sidecar, tried to help. I pointed at my map indicating where we wanted to go. The taller skinny one pointed and said something. If it was "don't go there," we were in trouble.

By some miracle, we arrived at the Czech border, showed our passports, and learned that we didn't need the windshield sticker required for cars. The problem was that I couldn't detect any consistent rule about which lane to use. Taxis darted in out as if the two-lane road was three across. The imaginary middle lane apparently belonged to the driver who was least chicken. It was an insane Czech version of the Texas Pass.

Another problem navigating was that the drivers seemed to have the horn and brake pedal confused. I swear that when they meant to slow down they honked instead. The more immediate the need to stop the longer the horn blared.

In addition to the crazy traffic, it looked like Tijuana, Mexico. Ceramic pots, beer, colorful blankets, and hookers lined the streets. Something for everyone to buy.

WILLING WOMEN LINED the road, their big legs covered in mesh stockings. More leaned out from second-floor windows showing huge cleavage, even from a distance. I lifted my face mask. "It looks like Mexico!" I hollered, not knowing he was thinking the same thing.

It was noisy. Dusty. Dirty. But leaving the border town it grew peaceful. Sunflowers wilted in the heat. Toast-colored mountains of hay rose like loaves of bread from a giant's bakery.

IN THE COUNTRYSIDE, traffic was light except for lumbering, ancient farm vehicles. They must have been some Russian variety because although I spent my working life in the car business, I'd never seen the likes of these.

Nearing Prague, we spotted a sign to The Yacht Club Caravan Park and followed the arrows.

ACCESS TO THE campground was on a Huck Finn type raft with a motor. Calling it a "ferry" implies a schedule that did not exist. In theory, it made the two-minute run to the island on the hour but we learned that it depended on whether the boat man was drunk or sleeping it off.

We set up our tent near a couple from Denmark who later put a large Denmark sticker on our saddle bags without asking. Rick had liked them until they pulled that stunt. He was meticulous about the placement. Each was thoughtfully chosen by size and style. Our saddle bags were becoming works of art and I was surprised that after a short burst of angst at the unrequested addition, he let it slide and didn't remove it.

A friendly older couple from Milan, Italy, were on the other side of us and their friendship proved invaluable helping us navigate the Prague transit system.

A CLUSTER OF tiny European fifth wheel RVs were parked nearby. Christie said they looked like fifth wheels for Barbie and Ken dolls. The micro-trailers had towing brackets on the roofs of the cars that looked about as substantial as ski racks. No 40-foot loaded rigs here.

JULY 17 A ride with our boat man, bus to town, and a few minutes on the underground, designed by the Soviets, and we were in old town Praha.

THE VENDING MACHINES that sold subway passes were complicated and I was willing to skip it and ride for free. If it hadn't been for the help of our camp mates from Milan, I might have ended up in the Czech version of transit mall prison. They showed up, offered to help, and, knowing which buttons to punch, got us our passes. A few minutes later when I got off the subway, a man in uniform stopped me and demanded to see my ticket. Thanks to our new pals from Milan, I had one. A close call.

Fifteen bridges cross the River Vltava. Prague's population is well over a million. Its cathedral took 600 years to build. But numbers alone don't describe Prague. Everywhere we walked, pastel buildings were surrounded by statues and frescoes. It was an artist's dream and I wished I could prop up an easel and capture the magic. But I'm a writer and all I could summon was, "Pinch me. This can't be real." We took twice as many pictures as anywhere else.

A VAST COURTYARD, about twenty football fields across, was covered in hand-laid stonework and surrounded by shops and restaurants. A web of streets spanned in all directions. We sat at a table and ordered soup and beer. Warm, thick, and filling. Tall, dark, and cold. And cheap.

A crowd was forming in the courtyard. Turns out it happens at the top of every hour. A skeleton struck the hour of the 1400s astronomical clock on the side of the Town Hall Tower. While it chimed, a trap door opened and an image of Christ marched out ahead of his disciples.

When the show was over, we moved closer to see the figures flanking the clock. They represented the four things that were despised at the time. Vanity, greed, death, and pleasure. "I can accept disdain for the first three, but no pleasure?" I said, thinking how much I'd enjoyed the beer, soup, and low price. And my wife and this trip. All pleasures.

We walked across the Charles Bridge, past the blackened-by-age statues, Gothic towers, and arches. It was more like a street carnival than a bridge walk. Tiny puppets dressed in peasant clothes danced, kissed, and pranced on an itty-bitty stage. We had no idea what the plot was but it drew an enthusiastic crowd. The bridge is long and we spent nearly an hour getting across, stopping to watch artists at work and to toy with vendors who thought we might buy.

I did make one vendor happy and scored some spouse points when I negotiated a price for a gold chain for Christie. She resolved the customary "where will we pack it?" question by snapping the clasp around her neck.

PRAGUE WAS THE first place I'd been so tempted to shop. Glassware in brilliant colors, garnet jewelry in a variety of blood-red shades, and elaborate cloisonné vases and pitchers all caught my eye. I chose an egg-shaped green and blue cloisonné pendant and happily hung it from my new necklace.

PRAGUE CASTLE IS the largest in the world and dates to the 9th century. It's always been the seat of Czech rule as well as their official residence. The castle was a mind-boggling line-up of museums and monasteries. The Imperial stable, a convent, St. Vitus Cathedral, the powder tower, Vladislav Hall, and even a toy museum.

WE WANDERED THE Royal Gardens where Emperor Rudolf II had his zoo. Tiny colorful houses built into the arches of the Castle walls were souvenir shops but in the 17th century, goldsmiths lived in them. We walked down a staircase that knights on horseback had ridden on their way to jousting matches.

WITH NO REAL agenda, we found ourselves in the Jewish sector, just outside the walls of Old Town. Jews first came to Prague in the 10th century but in the 16th century, the neighborhood called "Josefov" was walled in at the direction of the Pope, who declared that Jews and Christians shouldn't live together.

In the synagogue, the names of 77,000 who died at Auschwitz were listed.

"Christie," I said, running my finger down a column of names. "Whole families were wiped out." The fact that the Nazis tried to exterminate a whole race was horrifying and the evidence of what

Hitler and his disciples did was right there in front of us. Names on a wall.

"It's hard to accept," she said in a voice so quiet I could hardly hear.

Surprisingly, Hitler planned to preserve Josefov to show the world what the Jews looked like and how they lived before he annihilated them.

BUT THE RESULT is very different. Josefov today was very much alive. In the marketplace I bought a metal platter painted in bright colors, showing the town's skyline. It was unbreakable, would pack flat and I'd use it as a campsite tray. Handing the man a few bills, he told me he used his profit to support the cause of maintaining the memory of how evil works when good people are silent.

Playbills were shoved in our hands at every turn. I longed to be in Old Town at night so we could go to a concert but the unpredictability of the "ferry" meant we had a self-imposed back-before-sunset rule. We were like teenagers with a curfew so the music offerings would have to wait for a different kind of trip.

CHRISTIE KEPT DODGING into the shops and I had to keep a close eye so we didn't get separated. We had a standing agreement. If we couldn't find each other we were to go back to the place we were last together. If that failed, we'd return to the bike. Fortunately, it hadn't happened yet and it was day 46.

At an antique instrument shop, dusty violins, mandolins, and horns crowded the shelves. The owner had played for the Czech president and toured America, playing in Austin, Texas, and Washington DC. Now, in Prague, he played for us, an audience of two.

A sign caught my eye. An apartment in Old Town on the main square was for rent, $1300 a month. Checked it out. In the newer part of town and in the outskirts, rents ran $300–$400 a month. "Nice place and good price. But we don't speak the language," I said to the real estate man, who did speak some English.

WE TALKED ABOUT staying. We'd lived on our sailboat and then in an Airstream trailer ever since the girls had left home. They'd both long since graduated from college but was I ready to end seven years of rootlessness? I wasn't sure.

Rick said, "I love Prague but I'm pretty sure I'd never feel at home here."

"I know. Me, too. And I haven't seen any golf courses either." I did know my husband. We thanked the real estate agent for his time and said good-bye.

WAITING FOR THE boat to take us to the campground, we saw rats poking at garbage at the edge of the water. We hollered across the river for nearly half an hour, trying to get the guy's attention. The scurrying rats made it feel longer. When our boat man finally arrived, he offered to take us to the campground for a 50-cent tip. We didn't have much choice.

We spent the evening reading *USA Today*, sipping wine from coffee cups, and doing laundry.

I HAD NO idea there could be so many versions of washing machines. Here, the drill was to first ask the owner to unlock the laundry room. Once we'd gained entry, we attempted to decipher the instructions. Before we could make much progress, the small room was crowded with "helpers," fellow campers who knew how the machines worked. All of them were smoking and waving their arms. One took our bundle of clothes. Another the soap. A third picked coins from Rick's outstretched hand. It reminded me of the scene in

Fiddler on the Roof when the sewing machine arrived. Sometimes it does take a village.

JULY 18 Packed up and loaded, we said goodbye to our friends from Milan, the Danes with the huge sticker, and Monica and Mats, Swedes from an Arctic Circle town, population 29. At their next village meeting they said they were going to tell about the Americans they'd met in "da Praha camping."

As WE WERE pulling away, a man in a pale blue bathrobe ran toward us, waving maps and brochures. He was from Belgium and spoke English with a French accent. From the pictures he held for us to examine, we figured he, too, wanted us to visit his home. But he was suggesting a Czech town we should visit. Cesky Krumlov. It looked interesting and we decided Austria could wait.

A sober ferry man took us across the river. Rick filled the tank with "natural gas," the name for unleaded gas in Czech. The signs were easy to follow and we rode south into hilly countryside.

I wrote in my little notebook while Rick drove. "I'm inspired as I haven't been since Ireland. The countryside is clumps of evergreens, rolling wheat fields and corn. Clusters of tile roofed buildings with red onion shaped domes surprise me around each bend."

A billboard read, "Do Ameriky." I found out it meant, "Fly American Airlines."

STOPPED FOR LUNCH at a swank-looking restaurant with waiters in bow ties and white shirts. Tables were family style so we joined a group at a large table. Meat and potatoes, coffee and gingerbread. $8 for everything including a generous tip.

Cesky Krumlov is a medieval village with a river running through it. I parked in a cobblestone square, in front of a shrine. Christie and I struck out separately, scouting for lodging. For how many nights, we had no idea. There were lots of choices. We met back at the bike and after a brief comparison of amenities and prices, agreed on where to stay.

CESKY KRUMLOV IS a UNESCO World Heritage site built on hills with long flights of stone steps. With no idea what to see or where to begin, we chose to go left because it was downhill. The narrow lane followed the banks of the Vltava River, past 15th- and 16th-century stone buildings.

JULY 19   A 13th-century fairy tale castle sat like a crown at the top of the town. With pointy turrets as toppers, it looked like a multi-tiered wedding cake frosted with peach and raspberry sherbet.

BUILT IN THE 1200s, it's the second largest castle in Europe and guarded by a dry moat with bears living in it. Real bears! They're said to be descendants of the original bears that have guarded the castle since the early 1700s. We joined an English language tour.

THROUGH ROOM AFTER room we trailed behind our young, chubby guide in her too-tight skirt and rumpled white blouse. She struggled with the English language and it was a valiant effort. I certainly couldn't give a tour in any language except my own and I felt sorry for her when three mouthy teacher-tourists pelted her with trivial questions.

Thick, silky rugs lay over sofa backs and a French clock delicately painted with pastoral scenes and edged with gold ticked emphatically. The tallest of our three annoying tour members wanted to know how often the clock was wound. I couldn't take it any longer and scooted forward, next to the three.

"You know," I said conspiratorially, "I heard there's a test at the end for everyone who asks questions. I don't know what they do to the people who fail it." I dropped to the back of the group, rejoining Rick, who was laughing behind his brochure. The threesome was mute for the rest of the tour.

Leaving the castle was downhill; we walked over and around the river in cobbled switchbacks. We stopped on a bridge to watch boat loads of vacationers playing in the rapids. But we both needed haircuts so we went in search.

FOR $2.50, A blonde lady barber gave me a #1 all-over buzz and my first manicure. I looked like a Marine recruit with nice nails.

WE TOOK A table for lunch on a patio overlooking the river. While waiting for our goulash, we chatted and munched on hard pretzels hanging from spindles on a wooden stand in the middle of the table.

An elderly gent seated a few tables away half-rose out of his chair and hoisted his beer in our direction. "You must be from Texas," he called in our direction. He had just a few threads of grey hair on his bald head and must have overheard our American accents. "I remember," he continued. "You came in 1945. And freed us." We weren't from Texas. In 1945 Rick was two and I hadn't been born. We smiled and raised a pretzel to meet his toast. But we didn't know what to say. We were, quite literally, speechless.

The weather was warm and sunny. We watched the river flow over and around rocks much as it probably had in the 1940s. I fingered the cloisonné bauble hanging from my new gold chain and ran it back and forth, like a worry bead.

The goulash was good but we'd lost our appetites, subdued by the fact that a war that had receded in the minds of most Americans was obviously still fresh for our fellow diner.

Our lunch bill included a charge for each missing pretzel. We had a much needed chuckle over that.

NOT FAR AWAY, a display of children's artwork hung on a 14th-century stone wall. Little plaques told us each young artist's name, birth and death dates. All girls. The drawings were of stick figure families, sunshine, and trees. Colorful and timeless, they were typical of children's drawings everywhere.

Most had been 10 to 14. A couple of older ones lived for a few more years. One was still alive. They were all Jews, killed by the Nazis, and we surmised that the girls who lived were mostly used as prostitutes.

We turned away and walked a short distance. Seated on a bench, tears flowed easily. I felt the surge of what so many young men must have felt when they rushed to enlist. I wanted to kill some Nazis.

> *"There are two kinds of light – the glow that illuminates, and the glare that obscures."*

> – JAMES THURBER (1894–1961)

CHAPTER 10

BAD ISCHL TO BAD KARMA

JULY 20 Entering Austria, we bought the obligatory highway permit and stuck it on the windshield. Smooth highways weren't the only change. Homes were handsome and perfectly kept. Affluence was obvious.

It was a motorcycle rider's alpine fantasy. Winding roads, sparkling lakes, and granite cliffs that disappeared in the clouds.

A series of tunnels led us to Hallstatt, a salt mining town since 1200 BC. Historians estimate about 10,000 tons of salt passed through the valley each year in medieval times.

We rented a room above Hallstatt's pizza restaurant and followed the directions to the room. When I opened the door, I thought we had the wrong place. Its acreage looked like a community meeting room. The travel gods had delivered us to a four-room apartment with a living room large enough for a dozen people to dance. We stocked up at the market and planned to eat-in since our home was a veritable mansion.

HALLSTATT IS SO tiny you could explore it in ten minutes but we took an hour. Uniform chocolate-colored chalet homes all had red and pink geraniums flowing from their window boxes. "Perfection must be required by law," I said to Rick.

A waterfall crashed to the street below, rushing between the houses, under the road and into the lake on the other side. Trees stood like church spires. The way the forested hillside dove straight into the lake, it looked like a fjord. A train spewed steam on the opposite side. Swans glided and ducks paddled around them in little circles. Low-hanging clouds hung like vapor puffs. We kept walking.

A SIGN EXPLAINED that the Nazis had dumped valuables in the lake and hidden more in the tunnels used to transport the valuable salt. The stash included counterfeit U.S. money and arms as well as stolen art and jewels. Much of it was eventually recovered and donated to the Simon Wiesenthal Center in Los Angeles.

We looked for Beinhof, the House of Scrolls. It was closed but we explored a small church and the cemetery in back. The headstones were works of art.

MULTIPLE GENERATIONS SHARED a single burial space. I thought about Rick's parents: one buried in Colorado and one in Arkansas. One of our daughters lived in Oregon, the other in New York City. I couldn't imagine my family being buried with a single headstone or even within 1,000 miles of each other.

At the back of the property, in a pocket of shadows, I stumbled. When I recovered my balance if not my dignity, I looked down. There at the side of the path was a pile of skulls and bones. "Oh, that's gross," I said, shuddering and walking backward. "Why do you think they're here?"

"Maybe the family members didn't pay the cemetery so they exhumed the bodies," Rick offered as a possibility.

That was an explanation for the mummies at Museo de las Momias in Guanajuato, Mexico anyway.

One aspect of independent travel is that our questions often went unanswered. There was no one to ask and we didn't speak the language anyway. I reminded myself that I didn't necessarily need an answer to every question. Here or at home.

To TOUR THE salt mine, we rode a funicular up the mountain where we were issued bulky overalls to tug on over our clothes. They were attractively equipped with a heavy leather crotch that hung low, especially on the shorter gals.

In groups of six, we straddled logs and shot downhill through a narrow tunnel. An 80-year-old woman from Ohio sat in front of me and Christie was in a different group. Climbing off the logs, we continued our descent into the world's oldest salt mine on a series of park-like slides. It wasn't an E-ticket thriller but it was pretty unique.

WHERE SALT CAME from had never crossed my mind. I'd used the expression "back to the salt mines," but in jest. Here, I learned the importance of salt beyond breakfast eggs. Hallstatt salt is used on roads, in medicine, make-up, glass, and aluminum. Only 10% of what is mined is for food additives and table salt.

JULY 21 When our time in Hallstatt was over, I got careless walking the bike up the gravel driveway and dropped it. I was really angry with myself and I admit I probably showed it. "Get a grip," I muttered, trying not to get too worked up.

"GET A GRIP" is not what Rick said. He was walking the bike up the gravel driveway and it was really much too heavy to be a reasonable thing to do. He dropped it on its right side; it got a few scratches. I didn't see what the big deal was.

"A bike needs to be flawless," he thundered.

"Then park it in a closet," I spat back.

We climbed on and rode away, minus our good moods. I thought about the furniture that had gotten scarred during our many family moves. Lampshades dented. Furniture and artwork scratched. "Shouldn't household goods be more pristine than a vehicle?" I thought. Apparently not, because Rick had always taken those screw-ups in stride. "Must be a Venus-Mars thing," I decided and settled into my seat behind Rick, remembering to breathe.

Bright green hillsides reached straight upward. The valleys were dotted with the same dark brown chalet homes splashed with geranium boxes at every window. A tall church spire, a ski lift, and ten minutes later another town with all the same postcard images.

THE ALPS. MOTORCYCLE heaven. From mountain to valley, we wound our way through the passes.

In Kitzbuhel, a banner ran across the main street announcing a major tennis tournament. That was intriguing and the campground checked most of the good boxes: near town, large plots, lots of grass. Expensive, though. This one was $23 a day and we were used to paying in the $10 range. Camped next to us was a handsome couple from Australia who were exploring Europe as we were but in a rented station wagon.

"Now that makes sense," I said to Christie. "Sometimes I wish we'd leased a car."

THE AUSSIES' TENT was larger than we could carry and they had folding chairs. I had serious chair envy. But, a car? He had to be kidding. "I thought those passes were pretty incredible," I said. "You did have fun riding them, didn't you."

"Well, yeah," he looked a bit sheepish. "But when it rains a car would be nice."

Our jeans could nearly stand up on their own so we sought out the laundry room. While our clothes got macerated in soap and water, we went to a barbecue dinner in the campground. We shared a picnic table with a group of Australians and two couples from Belgium. An accordion player and dancers in lederhosen entertained us.

One gal at the table told me a cautionary tale. She knew a couple who were riding a mountain pass in a rain storm when it turned to sleet. "When your partner's helmet begins to change shape," she said, "that's ice. Stop immediately." I swore to remember, hoping I wouldn't need to.

JULY 22 I crawled out of the tent to bright blue sky and warm sunshine; a perfect day to hike from Kitzbüheler Horn to Eichman Lift. We filled our day packs with lunch, snacks, and water and rode the bike to the tram parking lot where I bought a fistful of tickets. We would ride two ascending lifts, another one part way down and, of course, the bus ride back to the parking lot.

STANDING ON TOP of the world, gentle breezes played with the trees below. We walked in single file with a half dozen fellow hikers across an impossibly green meadow dotted with purple and yellow flowers. A red butterfly flitted by. I stepped off the trail and turned in a slow circle. We were surrounded by soaring granite peaks. In the second hour of walking, we passed jeweled lakes and hurrying streams that we navigated by leaping between boulders.

Passing lederhosen-clad hikers greeted each other, calling out, "Grus Gott." It meant "Go with God," which seemed appropriate. It was heaven. I liked saying it, too, but Rick stuck with the American version. He smiled and waved, saying "Hi there" for every "Grus Gott."

THE NARROW TRAIL was well marked and there were lots of sheep, of course. Water gurgled in the fast-moving creeks and cow bells clanged. It really was mountain music. We'd been told that Austrians not only have the shortest work week in Europe but also the longest life span. Their attitude toward good living is called *gemütlichkeit*. I couldn't begin to pronounce it but I liked their "embrace the moment" attitude.

When it couldn't get any better it got decadent. We came to a *kneippen*, a rectangular snow melt pond, fenced off from the cows. A hiker's foot bath. All this beauty and a mid-hike foot massage, too? How civilized. Seated on log benches, we raced to get our dusty laces untied.

WEARING JUST MY shirt and underwear, I took tentative steps into the icy water. The magic was in the pebbles at the bottom and I submerged my overheated body. Wiggling my toes in the gravel, I moaned like a woman in the throes of passion.

I'M NOT A fan of cold water but I did submerge myself and enjoy it. It was Christie's sounds of pleasure that made the cows curious and they turned to "moo" back at her.

WE'D BEEN ON the mountain for six hours when we came to the lodge where we'd catch the descending lift, a single wide. Alone, I hung suspended on a cable above a brilliant green meadow, splash-painted by wild flowers. The music of cow bells floated on the crisp air, mingling with church chimes.

IN THE PARKING lot, a para-sailor came in for a landing within a few yards of the bike. He expertly landed next to the trunk of his car, packed up his chute and drove off without a word. Fun to watch such expertise but it wasn't on my list.

It was sufficiently difficult to keep the loaded bike upright, often at speeds over 80 mph. Adding too much rain and foreign signage provided plenty of challenge.

JULY 23 Sunday morning in Kitzbuhel was quiet with the stores closed. Christie window-shopped the high-brow shops but what I ogled was parked next to the curb. A half dozen Porsches were between a silver Maserati and a red Ferrari. Across the street sat a pristine yellow Lamborghini. Not a Fiat in sight. A snazzy BMW model I'd never seen before sped by. It wasn't even a car show, just a Sunday morning in Kitzbuhel, Austria.

RICK COULD HAVE spent all morning looking at the parked cars but we had tickets to the tennis tournament. The courts were red clay and the commentary was in both English and German. The action was high paced and dramatic.

We gawked at the sponsor tents: Nike, Nordica, Mercedes Benz, and random racquet manufacturers. Not being able to read the signs gave me a sense of what it might be like to be illiterate. Separate and clueless. The language barrier put us in a bubble of non-information but I didn't mind.

JULY 24 Headed for Dachau, we chose a back road to take us from Austria into Germany. We arrived mid-afternoon and for the first time, couldn't find a place to stay. No rooms, no camp-grounds, nada. I stopped at every hotel, gasthaus and zimmer. A dozen times, Christie got off, checked on availability, and came back shaking her head.

"Can they all really be full?" I asked.

"I don't get the feeling there's any big event in town or anything," she replied, climbing back on. "It's more like they don't want us to stay. It's kinda creepy. I feel about as welcome as a Black traveler in the deep south in 1940."

IT WAS TEMPTING to leave but being told that "there's no room in the inn" was having the opposite effect. We dug in our collective heels. On the outskirts of town, near a strip mall, we found a chain motel, like a Super 8, that had a room. We stored our gear and rode back to a camping store Rick had spotted during our room search.

I NEEDED NEW boots. The tread on the used ones I'd started with had worn thin. A BMW is tall and even though I'm nearly six feet tall, my legs are relatively short. Thicker soles would help me balance the bike when we were stopped and when Christie got on. At a Fritz Berger shop, I bought a pair of Lowa Gore-Tex® boots and left the old pair in the room, a gift to whoever ended up with them.

WE GOT SOME ice from the motel bar, a plastic sleeve of eight cubes the size of gingersnaps. Some things just make you laugh. Or was it that I needed a good laugh in order to shake off the creeping depression that was Dachau?

JULY 25 At the entrance a sign read, "Work will make you free." My father had preached the work ethic my whole life. He admonished that success came from his creed, "Be early,

be honest." But the concept that work made you "free" didn't sit well. Ask slaves. Work wasn't going to save the Jews, gypsies, political opponents, and other "undesirables" in Nazi Germany but that's what the sign said.

Low clouds hung like heavy drapes but the sun was trying to peek through. We walked through the gates. The air was still, like an indrawn breath.

I LOOKED OVER the glossy brochure I'd been handed. The Dachau Camp was in operation from 1933 to 1945. Over 200,000 people were imprisoned here. An Aryan guide led us through the barracks. Plaques indicated that prisoners were used for medical experiments but the guide's cheerful tone belied that truth. She told us that "those who died here expired because of 'starvation, exhaustion and disease.'" Not torture, firing squad, or incineration.

"Dachau had a gas chamber," the guide said in a chillingly cheerful tone, "but it wasn't used."

SHE SPOKE IN heavily accented English, explaining the meaning behind the pictures and exhibits in what I called a "museum-voice." Her high-pitched delivery dished out details like meringue on pie.

"Why is this place so cleaned up?" I wanted to ask. "So the Germans won't feel guilty about what they let happen?" My eyes blurred with tears.

Bars of sunlight latticed the ground. I rolled my Prague pendant between my fingers, sliding it back and forth along the chain, and dabbed at my eyes. Defying our guide's chipper instruction to "keep up now people," I moved at the pace of a bank vault door. Shuffling along, I thought about the superior attitude it takes to define who is "inferior."

THE TILED ROOM had an overhead sign that read "shower room." There was an oven in the middle. The ovens were for the purpose of "incinerating the bodies of those who had already died," we were told. She said the word "ovens" as though chocolate chip or walnut-raisin had been baked there. History says that at least 40,000 were exterminated at Dachau.

"AS THE WAR was ending, the prison ran low on fuel," she said. "When they could no longer burn the bodies, it was the stench that led those living nearby to investigate." I was furious. Hello? They believed this death camp was a prison; hence, their innocence? My father had taught us to take responsibility for our actions, too bad he wasn't the mayor of Dachau.

A sign at the exit, read, "Thanks for visiting." The banal message hit like a fist. Dachau had been whitewashed and sugar coated. I was outraged. But the good news was the numbers of European teenagers touring, too.

"The young people will help future generations remember," Rick said as we left. I prayed he was right.

MY NEW BOOTS made it easier to balance the bike. With both feet firmly on the ground, instead of just my toes, I felt much more secure when Christie got on.

I drove slowly through town, passing faded pastel buildings and a church shaped like a child's drawing. After four hours of wading through blood, we needed a break. Patches of blue sky helped my mood and I stopped at a street market.

Dachau looked quite prosperous and the marketplace was pleasant but bad karma felt like a heavy blanket on my shoulders. The stench of atrocity had an acrid smell seven decades after the fact.

I DIDN'T NEED to buy, just to breathe the scent of fresh flowers and drying herbs. We watched ladies filling the baskets over their arms with pastries, fruits, and vegetables. Like mouthwash after eating liver, I was reviving.

JULY 26   We rode all day through one picturesque town after another. Rows of grapevines climbed the hills and their symmetry appealed to me. Corn stood tall. Sunflowers smiled. Geranium-clad window boxes perched on every sill as if we were still in Austria.

We rode the Romantikstrasse (Romantic Road) to Rothenberg, a medieval walled town. A campground below the wall caught my eye and we rode down to examine it. I would have booked a month if we'd been able to sit still that long. Rick spied a few abandoned trailers on the property that he said "didn't look inhabited." I had no idea how he could tell but at his suggestion, I asked if we could have a trailer instead of a campsite. The answer was "yes" for $1 more a day.

AND THAT'S HOW Campingplatz Tauber Romantik became "home."' We had beds, a little kitchen, and a radio! We even had chairs under a gnarled apple tree.

Rick Steves' guidebook said, "To hear the birds and smell the cows, take a walk through the Tauber Valley." Christie took that literally. Before we even unpacked, we took a walk. She'd spied a covered bridge over the Tauber River that needed exploring. It led to the village of Detwang, which is actually older than Rothenberg.

IT TOOK ONLY a short stretch of the legs to fall in love. A skinny castle. A thousand-year-old church. We walked through colorful gardens and back across the Tauber River.

Moving into the trailer was easy. Rick dumped everything from the saddle bags onto the kitchen table.

JULY 27 After a leisurely breakfast under our apple tree, we set off on the twenty-minute walk into Rothenberg. The walled medieval town is famous for its Christmas theme and Christie had holiday ornaments in mind.

Cobblestone streets. Dogs in restaurants. Old folks chatting on benches. It was a bit touristy with the reputation of being "Germany's best-preserved walled town" but we were staying in the village below so it didn't bother me.

In St. Jacob's church we examined the 500-year-old wood carved altar piece and climbed the stairs behind the organ.

The Museum of Criminal Justice was both horrifying and entertaining. Twelfth- to nineteenth-century methods for keeping society in line included diabolical devices like an iron cage, ridicule masks, thumb screws, pillories, stretching wheels, a gallows, and the rack. Swords, axes and an executioner's mask. No Miranda rights in those days. And I got a real laugh at the metal "nag gag."

Note: It's not a good idea to suggest its use just because your spouse is chatting more than you'd like.

In the main square, a raucous group of Texas college boys serenaded the tourists under an enormous cuckoo clock. The historic legend is that on the hour, if the little window opens and an image of the mayor pops out to drink a flagon of ale, the town will be saved. The fraternity boys seemed to be participating heavily and Rothenberg looked plenty healthy and not in need of rescue.

WHEN DUSK SETTLED over the walls, the bus loads of day trippers left and the post card shops closed. In the deserted moonlit streets, we joined a rollicking night watchman's tour and when it ended, we stopped for a bowl of stew. The iron table rocked on the uneven cobblestones but I didn't care.

The view stretched over the red-tiled roofs to the murky and mysterious moat beyond the wall. Maybe I'd been spooked by the stories the watchman told but for that moment, the cannons were loaded and torches illuminated the heads of bad guys on poles. With a dash of moonlight and a splash of wine, Rothenberg was a medieval crossroads again.

JULY 28   While our breakfast cooked, I put together a box to mail to the U.S. I filled it with a handful of postcards, four Christmas ornaments, an assortment of small gifts, and two filled journals. We mailed three such packages during our four-month ride.

TOOK OFF TO find a post office and to explore the Romantikstrasse. We hadn't seen many signs in English, so it surprised me to see *Romantic Road* in Japanese script. It was the first non-German language sign we'd seen in Germany. Tells you something about who visits.

The scenery was straight out of a vacation brochure. First stop was Dinkelsbühl. I parked and we explored yet another medieval village with the obligatory colorful buildings and hanging baskets of flowers.

ORNAMENTED BUILDING FACADES were in every pastel shade on the color wheel. Sunset orange, soft green, pale blue, safflower yellow. Street vendors displayed fruit and vegetables, spices and baskets, scarves and pottery.

We chatted with an English-speaking shop owner who told us, "Germans travel away from Germany on holiday because the spirit here is negative. Our land is lovely but our people make it ugly." We bought camembert and cucumber sandwiches on crusty bread and rode on thinking about what he'd said.

ATE OUR PICNIC at a roadside table and stretched out in the grass for a siesta before continuing to Bad Mergentheim. At the castle, we took a conducted self-tour. A forbidding flight of stone stairs opened into a cavernous room with ornate ceilings. In the center was a dining table that stretched forever, looking as though it could seat everyone we'd ever met. And a vast display of doll houses. Miles of them.

Christie wasn't liking the guttural sound of the German language but I disagreed. A doll house is a *"PuppenSchnoopen."* How fun is that?

I'd been making jokes and providing Christie with comic relief since Berlin when I'd taken to calling streets *"Kremmer-SchnoozelFlippenFlossStrasse"* or a variation on the theme. I'd coined *"Floppin-schmmizer," "whinkel dimmers," "Schloozen with floozen"* and now I could add *"PoopenSchnoopen"* with a straight face because it actually meant something in German.

BACK HOME, THUNDER cracked and rain pelted our little metal trailer. Lightning flashed like light bulbs but we stayed inside, playing cards and listening to the radio with a dinner of cheese, garlic toast, pâté and sour cream herring. Rick played with the German language while he rinsed the dishes, making me laugh. When a song came on the radio with a beat we enjoyed, we danced in the narrow space.

"Strange travel suggestions are dancing lessons from God."

– KURT VONNEGUT, JR.

CHAPTER 11
THE "KUR" AND THE CLIMB

JULY 29   At 100 mph the view was a blur. Rick was a man on a mission. He'd been talking about Friedrichsbad, the historic spa, since he'd read about it back in Tucson. I only hoped it would live up to his expectations.

NEAR THE FRENCH border, Baden-Baden was a playground for Europe's high-rolling elite 150 years ago. Royalty and aristocracy came to gamble in the classy casino and take the *Kur*, sauna and massage. My enthusiasm for the "cure" wasn't that it was historic but that the baths were coed and nudity was required. And a long soak would be good for us both.

We stopped at an inn with a "Welcome Bikers" sign but it was full and he recommended another. By luck and a few wrong turns we found it and moved into an ugly room. Before Christie could object too much, we took the bus back into town to find the spa. She'd stuffed our swimsuits, lotion, and hairbrush in a backpack but I hoped we wouldn't need the suits.

Paid $35 each for the full treatment but, of course, with all the signs in German, we weren't really sure what we'd signed up for. I was sent in one direction and Christie in another. She gave me a half-hearted wave, disappearing down a hallway following a no-nonsense German woman.

I FOLLOWED THE box in a uniform into a steamy world of marble columns. She pointed to a locker and gestured that all my clothes went there. I self-consciously stripped while she stood just feet from me, hands on her ample hips. I'd left my Prague necklace with my passport so it didn't take long to get naked. The gestapo brusquely snapped my locker shut and looped the key bracelet around my wrist. That's all I wore for the next four hours.

She ushered me to a warm shower which ended when she turned the dials to a rousing cold rinse. When her thick arm with blunt cut nails reached for the dial again, I went rigid just as a blast of hot water pelted me.

Following her down the hall, I obligingly stood with my arms out and legs spread in the airport security position. She and a woman who could have been her twin administered a rough soap and brush massage followed by a sharp spank. The swat seemed to mean they were through. An arrow pointed to a doorway.

Alone, I walked into a thermal steam bath. The air was thick with moisture but warm like a blanket. Gentler hands led me to a table. Flat on my back, I was vanilla fudge on the marble slab. The only sound was muffled doors opening and the steady hiss of steam being pushed through the vents. In a dreamy state, I thought about the curative powers of the waters. And wondered where in the vast building Rick might be.

Being naked was erotic at first but gradually it became simply sensual. The first hour blended into the second and I grew introspective and luxuriously self-absorbed. It was liberating. Pleasurable. Fun! At station ten I walked into a pool that was coed. Being over 50, I was less bothered by it than the 20-somethings in front of me.

OUR HALF-DAY SPA experience turned out to be 16 hedonistic stations that varied from pleasure rubs to scrub brushes. Under the dome of what they called the "Royal" pool, a coed crowd floated in the steam. A quick look confirmed that bodies come in more shapes than the imagination wants to think about.

I first spied Christie on the far side, seated next to a young American soldier. She saw me and swam over. We hugged, which felt good in the warm water. "Did you see the shape of that gorgeous thing at the far end?" she asked.

Oh my, she was right. A petite-in-all-the-right-places was as close to perfect as I've ever seen. Praise the Lord. And thank you, Christie.

I DIDN'T SEE any signs, that I could read anyway, saying I couldn't follow Rick out of the pool to the men's side so I did. I lay naked in the steam room with my eyes deliciously closed.

Later, back on the ladies' side, I sensed the end was near when I glimpsed the lockers. Two women rubbed lotion over every inch of my body, lingering nowhere. They ushered me, swathed in heated towels, into a sleeping room. Blanketed and prenatal, I slept.

MY GUIDE WRAPPED me in a warm blanket and laid me out prone on a narrow cot. Snoring rumbled through the semi-darkness in surround-sound and I joined in the chorus.

I WAS RELIEVED to see Rick standing near the exit door. We didn't say a word, just walked out into the rain.

Back in the "ugly room," it didn't look as bad. The lingering effects of the spa had mellowed me. I sat in the puke green velvet chair next to a lamp with a broken and bent shade. Rick sat on a brown bedspread whose history I shuddered to imagine. But it didn't matter. I pulled out my journal and Rick opened his book.

JULY 30 Rode a twisting highway into the famous Black Forest. A leak in my rain pants led to a wet crotch and I yearned for consistent dry weather and bright sunshine. Or better pants.

Passed through Freiburg and into the lake town, Titisee, for lunch. Rode on to Lake Constance and into Switzerland. Paid $30 for a Swiss highway pass, a sticker that goes on the windshield that authorized use of the highways for one year. We were cutting across Switzerland now but knew we'd use it when we circled back.

THE STORM GREW. Rain sprayed us like a car wash and wind bent the trees in half. We rode through Bodele, Egg, Au and Schoppernau to Warth. We should have stopped and camped but kept going. I was travel weary but completely enthralled by views of the Alps, waterfalls, storybook villages, a steam train, avalanche fences, more flower boxes, and snow tunnels.

A PICTURE BOOK ride with deep gorges, lakes, streams, ski lifts and an occasional modern shopping center. I was tired and cold but hadn't seen a logical stopping place so we kept going. It was a mistake. A 300-mile day was our outside limit and I'd surpassed it.

I was cranky setting up the tent. Loud music came from the pub tent and drunk German vacationers sloshed by in the rain.

WE WERE CAMPED in Füssen, Germany, next to the highway, with only some bushes separating us from road noise. Where we'd pitched the tent, the ground was rock-hard but the path to the bathrooms was a series of puddles.

Rick was in a temper so after a chicken dinner at the beer garden he went back to the tent alone. The relaxation we'd achieved at the spa had evaporated in less than 24 hours.

The campground was party-central. Grandmas, teens and toddlers sat side-by-side at long tables in the beer hall tents. When the lederhosen-clad musicians shouted, they stood on their chairs and without sloshing their mugs of beer and soft drinks, hoisted the tables over their heads, singing and laughing. Their exuberance was contagious and I wondered how it was possible that I'd grown up being what I thought of as happy without all this laughter.

JULY 31 The big deal at Füssen is mad King Ludwig's Castle. Getting in required standing in line to get an entry time, then finding the right gate at the correct time. Since we'd been traveling off the tourist grid, it was disorienting to be surrounded by people speaking English and organizing themselves in a concrete jungle of turnstiles and organized lines.

In the middle of tourist chaos, I breathed deeply, trying to relax into the spirit of Baden-Baden. I was partially successful.

Hohenschwangau was the childhood home of King Ludwig II of Bavaria and is still owned by the original family. We saw a film of Ludwig's life and our Bavarian guide led us through a second castle, Neuschwanstein. it was intended as a personal refuge for the reclusive, and according to most reports, increasingly insane, king. He never lived there but 6,000 people visit every day.

What I liked about Neuschwanstein was that it looked exactly like the one called "Sleeping Beauty's Castle" at Disneyland. Or Disneyland looks like it.

But we wanted a castle experience without crowds and gift shops so following another Rick Steves suggestion, we rode a short distance, had a picnic in Reutte, Austria, and began the steep climb up a forested hillside toward the ruins of Ehrenberg castle. Clambering over rocks and past grazing sheep, we scrambled under and over tree branches and rocks. Rick looked at me with skepticism.

"Sure beats the crowds at castle-mania but are you sure there's something at the top?" he asked.

"Hey, it's good exercise. If nothing's there we'll head back."

Struggling up the last 100 yards, we pulled ourselves over the ledge and Ehrenberg castle came into view. "Wow. When do you think this place was in full swing?" I said in Rick's direction. The question was rhetorical since he hadn't read anything about it but I kept forgetting he'd been more awake in school than I. He had an answer.

"In medieval times, when salt traffic was in its heyday, they built a complex of fortresses and castles. This was a piece of that puzzle. Beginning in the 14th century, the forts controlled traffic and levied tolls."

I left Christie with that thought and went in search of a bathroom. Given the tumble-down condition of the castle and the hour-long scramble through underbrush to get there, I didn't actually expect one. A tall rock or a wide tree would suffice. Before I found either, I came upon an elderly gent with a cane and a proper hiking cap. No way he climbed that hill, I thought. And right behind him was a gaggle of non-English-speaking tourists. And a garishly shiny purple tour bus. Christie was going to get a good laugh out of this. I chuckled to myself at the absurdity of the climb we'd taken when there was a wide paved road up the other side.

I DECLINED RICK'S suggestion that we return on the paved road so we slipped and slid back down the way we'd come. The man we'd asked for directions on our way up three hours earlier was still tending his vegetable garden. His astonished look said, "Those dotty-looking Americans actually climbed the hill, saw the castle, and returned. Good to know not all of them need 5-star accommodations."

While I was busy being proud of us, Rick asked for advice on a nearby place to camp. "Gran," he said, pointing over his shoulder. I thanked him and walked to the bike cradling a dirt-spackled zucchini the size of a small baby in my arms.

AUGUST 1 The trip we'd planned with so much enthusiasm and naivete was half over. When I was cold, wet, and tired it seemed it would never end. But this morning the sun was shining and the sixty days we had left seemed like barely enough to see all we'd set out to explore.

We left the crowded Füssen campground early for the short ride to Grän, Austria. It was a full-fledged sunshiny day. Children were fishing. Swans gliding. The sky was filled with hang gliders hovering over the fields while we pitched the tent.

RICK THREADED THE supports into our sleeping mats, turning them into chairs. I plopped to the ground and leaned back appreciatively and I wrote in my journal, *"We're completely encircled by towering mountains. Daisies dance in the breeze. I have all day to enjoy it. All month if I choose."*

We walked into town but everything was closed from noon to 2:00 p.m. Went back later and I bought a pair of corduroy knickers and argyle knee high socks. I was feeling quite local.

CHRISTIE CONCOCTED A one pot dinner. Never quite sure what the contents will be when we buy the food packets. This one was a frozen bag that included rice, meat and gravy. Apparently the American law that requires the wrapper image to match the ingredients isn't universal. The vegetables in the photo weren't in the bag, so Christie rinsed the dirt off our German home-grown zucchini, chopped it up and dinner tasted pretty good washed down with a beer or two.

AUGUST 2 Crawling out of the tent I gasped when a cramp seized my left calf. When I straightened up and the cramp subsided, I thought, "Better a cramp in the leg than a cramp in the spirit."

We were certainly less comfortable than if we'd taken a traditional European tour but I felt exhilarated. Adventuresome. Happy. Lots of our friends, most of all my mother, would never understand and I didn't know how to explain it.

AT THE MARKET, Christie picked out bread, salami, and cheese. With sign language and lots of enthusiasm she got the groceries turned into sandwiches. She'd done it before, so I wasn't surprised that she got monstrous pickles and homemade cookies thrown in.

We hiked to the base of the gondola and bought round-trip tickets to the mountain top for $10 each. I felt a little wimpy when I saw our camp neighbor walking up

Gran Austria

WILDFLOWERS, COW BELL music, and breezes. Passing walkers called out the familiar "Gruss Gott." A 75-year-old couple told us that these were the "old Alps," which aren't as high as the "new Alps." At the mile-high shelter, Gosse Schlicke, I signed our names to the climbers' log. "Rick and Christie Gorsline, USA." We scanned the book back two and a half years; we were the only Americans.

FIVE HOURS LATER we descended to the village on the gondola. Along the rocky trail at the bottom, I was stopped by a road guard who wanted to collect a toll for using the stile to go over the fence. This gentle toll keeper was a cow, bell and all. She seemed pleased enough with licking the salt off my forearm.

OUR CAMPMATE, SABINE, was surprised that we were Americans. "I've been coming here all my life and never seen an American," she said. "How'd you find us?" We told her about the man with the zucchini.

Sabine had a PhD in music and planned to teach German and music. She was camping and hiking to think about divorcing a husband who didn't see a need to work. She was wrestling with what to do.

OVER A BOTTLE of wine, we dished out parental advice that was essentially about being true to her instincts. Christie and I took turns sharing our points of view for her to consider: divorce is sad but better than settling for an impossible marriage, better to make the painful change before there are children, and so on.

AUGUST 3 The campground that had been so idyllic in warm sunshine was now a puddle. Splashing into town, I joked, "This would have made a good boat trip."

"Yeah," Rick laughed. "Who knew we should have packed snorkels and fins."

THE DAY DISAPPEARED doing simple activities. We read, did laundry, explored Grän, and played cards for three hours at a pizza parlor. Hanging out in the restaurant led to a conversation with the cook. He spoke some Spanish so we used that as a communication bridge. He recommended a few good cycle rides in the Dolomites and we pledged to ride them with him in mind.

> *"If a man does his best, what else is there?"*
>
> – GENERAL GEORGE S. PATTON

CHAPTER 12

HANNIBAL TO THE *PASSEGGIATA*

AUGUST 4 Traversed the Austrian passes from Elmen to Imst. And I do mean "traverse." This kind of riding had a rhythm, like ski turns. Hopefully, without any mogul jumps because fog often obliterated the road. I felt the tension radiating across my shoulders.

THE PATCHY FOG was a blessing, at least for the passenger. It was only when the fog lifted that I could see how far we'd fall if Rick missed a turn.

RAIN AND FOG were cutting into the pleasure, so we skipped riding a second pass. Opting for the freeway, we bypassed Innsbruck and rode through another dozen Alpine villages that meandered over the Alps. But the temperature was dropping and it was hard to ride safely when my limbs were rigid from cold.

I'D NEVER SEEN SO much rain. It ran toward us, down the hill in scallops. Rick slowed and I knew he was concerned that we could hydroplane. I shivered despite the fact that I was wearing the fuzzy jacket I used as pillow stuffing, glove liners, and extra socks. Remembering the advice about freezing temperatures, I stared at the shape of Rick's helmet.

When it began to change, I leaned forward and forced my frozen lips to say, "Honey, your helmet's freezing."

He hollered back, "So are my fingers. This is a lousy idea."

Riding through a seven-mile tunnel, I leaned forward, lifted my face mask, and hollered, "This is great. It's like a blow dryer! A few laps in here and we might dry out." Rick just shook his head but his shoulders shook and I could tell he was laughing.

SINCE 217 BC, when Hannibal led his elephants and troops across the Alps, to modern times, the name "Brenner Pass" has been synonymous with adventure and intrigue. I'd read the stories and put the hammer down. We'd be there in thirty minutes.

After World War I, when international borders shifted, control of the pass was shared by Italy and Austria. During World War II, Hitler and Mussolini met on the pass to celebrate the alliance between between Fascist Italy and Nazi Germany. The pass was also part of the Nazi ratlines after the German surrender in 1945.

The 21st-century nod to so much history was just a McDonald's and a large parking lot. There weren't any elephants or reminders of the historic traffic that had navigated the route for 2,300 years but it was a welcome sight offering shelter and warm food.

I'M NOT A McDonald's fan in any language but I was happy to climb off and go inside. Rick and I took off our icy helmets and slung them over our arms. The building was warm and eating something familiar sounded pretty good, too. The burger I ordered came with whole peas and mashed carrots in the patty; so much for familiar.

After nearly an hour drying out and warming up we were ready to go again. Rick came out of the bathroom, pulling his soggy gloves back on. I asked, "How many ways are there to flush a toilet?"

He was tugging his helmet on and wiggling the ear pieces of his glasses into position. He laughed at my question and answered, "The one I just used whirled the seat around and pulled a squeegee in the bowl while water gushed down the sides."

"Yeah, the ladies had the same kind. Wasn't it in Cesky Krumlov that we cranked the water in manually with an old fashioned pump?"

"I think we had that kind in Rostock, too," he said.

"Yeah, I remember," I smiled, heading back out into the rain. "But my favorites are the bidets." I was looking down, trying to zip my wet rain jacket over soggy leathers.

"That's when it takes you longer to finish and you come out smiling, right?"

I hit him in the arm. "Enough potty talk. Let's go." We were still laughing when we climbed on the bike.

I STOPPED AT a toll booth on the Italian border and Christie paid. When the agent slammed the window shut, I started to drive away, thinking the transaction was complete

Christie yelled, "Stop. I didn't get any change."

The guy held a newspaper in front of his face and I could just picture his smug smile and my $12 in his pocket. After long minutes of pounding on the toll booth window and hollering, we gave up and chalked it up to Italian arithmetic.

Staying out of the way of the fast cars and dodging the slow ones, I ducked behind the windshield to hide from some of the rain. We needed to stop for longer than a burger break.

"It wouldn't take much for this to turn to snow," I hollered over my shoulder.

"I'll watch the shape of your helmet," she said, sounding nonchalant.

I reached back and patted her knee. A partner this good would be hard to replace and I reminded myself to drive carefully.

I SLOSHED TO the front door of a *zimmer*. The name alone should have told me that this far north in Italy, it was really Germany. A room price was "mit Frühstück," with break-fast. It was more than we wanted to spend for rainy, cold, Germany-in-Italy lodging. I was wet and depressed. I'd expected musical, cheerful, sunny Italy.

I DIDN'T CARE what it cost, we needed to be in a room with a shower and sheets. The place had a garage where we could leave Woody and lay out our wet gear. Christie would have to be patient with language and sunshine.

I told Christie, "Book it, Dano."

About an hour later, dressed in dry clothes, we walked to a market and returned with what could hardly be called dinner but met our needs. Settled in the room, we drank a bottle of wine and ate potato chips and ice cream for dinner. Boosted Christie's mood a bit and saved money, too.

AUGUST 5 Rick pulled the heavy drapes back, revealing clouds the color of milk and rows of vineyards right outside our window. I stayed in bed, caressing the smooth sheets with my feet.

Rick handed me a cup of strong dark coffee. Looking out the window, he said, "If 'less wet' is the new 'dry' we've got better days ahead." My enthusiasm was returning.

Riding out of German-Italy, vineyards stair-cased up the hills, disappearing into low clouds. We passed a yellow church and as Rick sped up, the vineyards became a blur of stout trunks and purple grape pyramids.

WE RODE PAST vineyards and through wet mist, headed for the jagged Dolomites. I looked forward to seeing Cortina, host of the 1956 Winter Olympics. For another hour the turns were as tight as the ones at motorcycle school. Villages strung together like train cars and the obligatory geranium-filled window box rule still seemed to be in effect. Chair lifts to left and right. Christie shrieked with delight when we swooped under a single-track wooden overpass that I guessed must be for skiers.

CORTINA D'AMPEZZO, AT last. It was Aspen, Colorado with steeper mountains and Italian flare. I loved the way it sounded rolling off my tongue. "Cor Tina Dahm Pezzo." I said it as often as possible.

Everything we owned was wet and cold. I lusted to be warm and dry. For a whole week. At Tourist Information we got a list of apartment rentals but it didn't show prices. I bought a phone card and made some calls but we didn't have a return phone number and I couldn't find anyone who spoke English.

IT WAS A valiant effort on Christie's part but we checked into Camping Olympia for five days in a small room above the camp bathroom. It was indoors with beds, a sink, and a covered deck where we could use the camp stove. Pretty close to heaven at just $35 a night in the illustrious "Cortina d'Ampezzo," which sounded even snazzier the way Christie pronounced it.

As the sun set, I watched the rain pelt the tents below. Smoking a cigar, I counted my blessings. A roof over our heads. A rack where our gear could dry out. Clean sheets. Someone to share them with.

AUGUST 6   Sunday morning, a loudspeaker blared the particulars of an outdoor church service in the campground. We dressed quickly and went to sit on a bench in the back. Being lapsed Presbyterians, the Catholic service in Italian had no specific meaning but it was fun to people watch.

We spent the afternoon in town, sitting on the square, sipping very black coffee and reading the *London Times*. Three hours slipped by and occasionally the sun peeked out.

"Watch that couple over there," I nudged Rick and pointed with my eyes instead of hands to avoid being rude.

He looked up. "What?"

"Watch them talk to each other."

A COUPLE WHO looked like they'd stepped off the cover of *Condé Nast* were engaged in hand-to-hand conversation. Their voices were low and their jeweled fingers waved within inches of each other's faces. He sported perfectly creased pants and leather pointy-toed shoes; she, a tight leather skirt, lace blouse, and boots. They were nearly bumping noses and despite their emotion, arm waving, and prancing, the sweater over his shoulders and the shawl around hers stayed perfectly in place. Never had a conversation looked so physical. But we were in Italy.

I just shook my head and went back to my newspaper. Bless Christie for not letting me miss a thing.

WE DINED ON our camp porch with the music of Italian conversations floating up from the campground below. I arranged my Prague platter with cold roast beef, marinated mushrooms, artichoke hearts, langosta, and olives. A juicy peach, a tiramisu parfait, and wine completed the meal.

AUGUST 7 Clear blue skies and information from our Dutch neighbor about a hiking trail nearby gave us a plan for the day. Coffee, bread with jam and boiled eggs, and we were off. We tramped in the Dolomites for six hours and returned for a nap and a shower.

Back at Bourtange, our postcard photographer, Hermann, had mentioned the *passeggiata* where Italians get dressed to the nines and stroll for no purpose except to be seen. We rode into town to check it out.

True to his description, the fashionistas were decked out for Gucci photo shoots. Skinny suede pants, fur boots, and a gold ski jacket on a warm evening. Young and old, some dressed in knickers, a few with snakeskin boots, and lots of shiny tasseled loafers and snazzy hats. We were the only ones decked out in American motorcycle leathers.

The shops were open late, so we wandered. Christie found a frying pan she couldn't live without and I picked out more peaches. At an internet café, we caught up on news from home. No crises brewing so Christie could relax for another ten days or so.

WE HAD 26 emails from family and friends from our sailing years. S/v *Belvedere* was in Alaska, s/v *Orinoco Flow* in the Panama Canal. Lisa had a new teaching job. AmyJean was covering the political conventions for MSNBC. Ann was in Indonesia, s/v *Unicorn* in Santa Cruz, Jim and Diana on a motorcycle tour of the United States. Good to have a snapshot of what was going on in the lives of those we loved.

AUGUST 8 Italian sunshine could be habit forming. We had breakfast on our patio, gave Woody a bath, and did the laundry. There was no dryer so we hung our shirts, socks and underwear on a line strung above the bed.

While the laundry dried, we rode to the site of the 1956 Olympics ski jump. Stopped, of course, at a nine-hole golf course and hit a bucket of balls. Also had fun with a one-on-one loser-does-the-dishes putting contest.

A NATTILY ATTIRED golfer looked like he was giving a lesson to an immaculately turned-out woman. But he talked on his cell phone the whole time while her husband held the poodle. Not sure who benefited from the hour but it was fun to watch.

AUGUST 9 We rode to the base of RioGerr lift, parked in the empty lot, and headed up the side of the hill. While we were sitting on a rock to rest, a small antelope-like deer darted in front of us. We found out it was a *camoscio*.

WHEN WE'D HAD enough hiking, we agreed to turn back at the next bend but just around that bend was a huge building with a sprawling deck. The "beautiful people" draped themselves over the railings, lay on lounges, and grouped at tables, indulging in icy drinks and bites of food. I thought it was a movie set but we'd stumbled on Faloria, a *rifugio*.

By comparison, our clothes and day pack looked even shabbier. I reminded myself that this wasn't high school, it was okay to be inappropriate.

THE VIEW FROM the deck was impressive. I inquired about overnight lodging, fully expecting at least a three-digit price. But it was just $40. I went back to where Christie was people watching and she quite reasonably asked, "What's the catch? It should be four times that!"

We had a glass of wine, our favorite "thinking juice," and booked a room for the next night. It included not just breakfast but dinner, too.

AUGUST 10 We left Woody in the custody of our camp hosts and took the bus into Cortina and the funicular to Rifugio Faloria. At a cost of $25 round trip, I was glad we usually hiked but it was fun being the "pretty people,"' not just watching them.

WE SPENT THE day lounging on the deck and hiked the rest of the way up the trail. It felt spiritual, closer to God somehow. Pillows of white and patches of lapis blue filled the sky but in the distance, balls of black clouds huddled over the Tre Cime Mountains.

Back on the deck at the *rifugio*, I prompted Rick to talk about our itinerary. My thoughts were that Venice might be warm but probably crowded and expensive. Switzerland was a good option because, after all, this was a motorcycle trip and the Alps were there. Rick didn't see why we needed to know and picked up an abandoned copy of the *London Times*, effectively ending the conversation that really hadn't been one anyway.

Late in the afternoon, when the colors on the horizon intensified, the crowds left. The lodge looked like the kind of place you'd have to book months, or even years, in advance. But we dined alone at a window table by candlelight. It was just us and the staff of college kids. We ate what they did. Spaghetti, salad, wine and bread.

AFTER ICE CREAM and cognac, we headed for the door. Christie had talked about the possibility of star gazing but given that we were the only guests, I was thinking about an empty lounge and a little marital activity.

Danny, a Brazilian gal whose father was Italian, had served our meal. She very politely told us we weren't allowed to go outside until morning. I felt like a kid at camp. "Is lock down the reason no one spends the night here?" I snarled, very disappointed now.

"No, they go down for the *passeggiata*," she said sweetly. "We do lock down for your safety."

My safety. Really? Were they saving us from a wild animal encounter? Afraid we'd fall off the mountain? Danny and the rest of the staff disappeared. I tried the doors. We were locked in, with no choice but to go upstairs to our room.

Sex on the bed wasn't as much fun as under Italian stars but it was good.

AUGUST 11 After breakfast we rode the first funicular down, accompanied only by a half dozen full trash bins. The upward tram passed, crammed to its legal limit with tourists. Suited me fine to be out of sync.

Back at the campground, we got Woody out of hock.

"Where are we going?" Christie asked.

"I thought I'd just follow the front tire," I said.

Christie laughed, "OK, I'll be right behind you."

HEADED WEST THROUGH northern Italy, the roads were narrow, especially in the villages. In one particularly tight spot, the people on the sidewalks were looking up and pointing, so I looked up, too. Above the truck in front of us, a corner of the building was now a chunk of plaster dangling from rebar. A few horns honked and a couple of pedestrians turned themselves into traffic control but no one seemed terribly concerned. In just a few minutes and without the help of police or officialdom, the traffic sorted itself out and got moving again.

We didn't see any exchange of paperwork or anything that would indicate concern beyond, "Oh well, these things happen." Apparently, there was no need to determine guilt or assess responsibility. It was one of many reminders that the American way is definitely not the only way.

We followed the Paseo de Vino, the Wienstrasse. I didn't need a dictionary to translate; proof was in the fields of purple grapes almost close enough to pluck. We rode past cornfields, apple trees, and castles. Rick stopped and I paid the toll for the autostrada using exact change.

ROADS WERE GOOD across northern Italy but I was alert because the Italians indulged the urge to pass whenever they felt like it. I didn't try to keep up, as was advised in my early trip-planning reading. Besides, Christie would have my hide.

I turned toward Switzerland and stopped in medieval, walled, ancient Glurns. There was a campground on the river but the town looked super-touristy and crowded. By now, we were medieval-walled–ancient city veterans so we rode on.

"Our happiest moments as tourists always seem to come when we stumble upon one thing while in pursuit of something else."

– LAWRENCE BLOCK

CHAPTER 13

KING AND QUEEN

WE CROSSED THE border into Switzerland under deep blue skies with just a few wisps of clouds. A enormous Swiss flag signaled our arrival, its red field with a white cross looking just like the image on the backs of ski patrol jackets.

We were headed to St. Moritz but in Zernez, a sign to a National Park diverted us. I liked the looks of a campground near the village. It sat in the middle of an emerald green meadow at the foot of the snow-sprinkled mountains. Perfect.

CHURCH BELLS PLAYED a nearly constant melody while we set up the tent. A short walk along a stream led to Zernez, a town of only about 1,000. Since it's the gateway to Switzerland's biggest nature preserve, the town was busy with vacationing Europeans planning to hike every day.

A POSTER IN the pub announced a town festival and Swiss barbecue in a few days. It was a "Grillplausch" with Alphorn entertainment. I was eager to attend but Rick was skeptical about staying the extra couple of days. What he forgot was that I'd already decided.

AUGUST 12   The sun rose, causing the snow-covered mountains to glow pink against the dusky dawn sky. I sipped coffee and inhaled the pleasures of our sweet-smelling meadow. Packing for the trip, I'd worried that I'd miss music, since I couldn't pack any. But the wind whispered and rustled the grasses in a melodic cadence that was as soothing as a favorite Kenny G or Andrea Bocelli CD.

CHRISTIE CLAIMED HER scrambled eggs tasted better cooked in the fancy Cortina pan and I didn't argue. Our alpine meadow spread out in front of the tent like a ten-acre putting green. When it got really warm, I moved our ground level makeshift chairs into the shade.

AUGUST 13   The next day, we got motivated and rode the 30 km to St. Moritz. It was a good ride through a valley with a rushing stream just below the road. The water was cobalt blue from glacial runoff.

Entering the glitzy ski town, a taxi driver who might have been middle Eastern passed me and the bus in front, cutting us off and scaring the piss out of me. I might have been more understanding but he went by with all his fingers pointing upward. I caught him at a stop sign and raised my middle finger. Not wanting to destroy foreign relations, I hoped he understood that I was simply suggesting it might rain. I heard Christie hissing something about calming down, which I did in my own time.

The supermarket in St. Moritz looked like something from a future century. Sleek and ultramodern with a sweeping escalator. I'd finished my book the day before and was on the hunt for a replacement. I love to read and not just road signs and maps, but it wasn't easy keeping reading material on hand.

A used copy of Pat Conroy's *Prince of Tides* might not have been my first choice but Christie and I shared our books. When one of us got part way through, we tore it in half. Took up less space that way.

WE CHECKED OUT the shops. I longed for a cute hat but bought consumables instead. A jug of wine, three one-skillet dinners, cheese, oranges, muffins, juice, tomatoes, an avocado, and a jug of lemonade. I could stock-up because our saddle bags were empty and the campground had a refrigerator-freezer for the campers to use. It was a luxury we had only at this one campground.

ON THE RIDE back, we passed an equestrian event and a pasture filled with flowers. A serpentine climb took us over 2,383-meter Flüelapass. We stopped to admire the scenery and talked to some fellow bikers at the turnouts. Mostly Swiss and Germans and an older man on a pristine R100, 1985 model. He'd been riding for 40 years and still had the love. There were so many motorcycles it was like a parade riding into La Punt except they passed us as if we were on a Schwinn.

ONE THING I loved about being on a bike was the camaraderie. When bikers saw each other, they always gave a down low hand signal; it was like a fraternity handshake and I was a member.

Rick kept his eyes on the road while I admired snow-rimmed alpine lakes and fields of wildflowers. We stopped in Wiesen because it was too picturesque to ignore and had a picnic on a bench at Tiefencastel. An aqua river pooled into an emerald lake and spilled on.

"I'd love to own that scene in a painting," I said to Rick.

"I agree, it's pretty, but we don't have a wall to hang it on," he said.

"Thanks for reminding me," I laughed. But I was still conflicted between wanting a home and wanting to be free to travel.

Back on the bike I counted my blessings. Not owning that painting or the wall to hang it on might be a good thing. "Please, God. Don't let me settle for second-hand images when the real thing is out here," I murmured, keeping my eyes open so I could lean into the curves like a good back seat rider.

ON THE SECOND pass, Albula, rocky cliffs were still snow-covered but lots of blue and yellow flowers meant the short summer had begun. Through town after town the main roads were barely eight feet wide. Bright red flowers bulged from second-floor window sills. Church bells rang.

I stopped to check-out a golf course. With rental clubs the fee was $160 each. Easy to skip. Headed back to the tent with no golf. Wrote in my log, "*There are lots of moments, especially when it rains, when I envy that Australian couple touring in their station wagon. Today wasn't one of them. A motorcycle is the only way to experience the Alps."*

I COOKED DINNER over a coin-operated stove. Goulash and spaetzle. Shared dinner and a big bottle of wine with a couple from Venice, Italy. Went to bed early.

AUGUST 14 Walked to town and caught a bus into the National Park. The driver spoke no English and seemed to relish having no idea what we were asking. Since we were boarding his bus and clearly needed to know how much it cost, I didn't see why hand signals wouldn't suffice. Couldn't he just hold up a few fingers to indicate a price? So far, that unhelpful attitude was the norm in Switzerland. The campground manager, too, was a "speak German or I won't talk to you" kind of guy.

RODE THE BUS for fifteen minutes for $3 each. Never found out if that was the right price or not. The scenery and delightful fellow tourists put language on the back burner.

In the park, we took a steep path that followed a stream. Stopped for a herd of deer feeding in a pasture. While our white wine chilled in the stream we soaked our feet and ate grapes.

Explored an ancient mine where minerals were extracted from the 14th to 18th centuries. Passed a ruin of some kind. Signs were in German, French, and Italian so we figured out what we could, interpolated as best we were able, and wandered on. We hiked for 3 1/2 hours.

Back on the main road, we came upon a couple from the campground, Ann and Ian, from Edinburgh, Scotland. They bought us a beer and gave us a ride home. They were classic. He was dressed like an REI ad from ten years ago. The duo were talkative, educated, and we greatly enjoyed their company.

AUGUST 15   Woke up to cows mooing. Before our coffee water boiled, Ann and Ian appeared with their arms full. They were carrying their big comfortable chairs. Ann said, "so zat ye be a Keeng and a Queen for da day." For the rest of our stay, whenever they left the park, they delivered the chairs for us to use.

THE LAUNDRY DRILL was that first you made a reservation for a two-hour time slot, then bought a key to start the washer. It took two hours for one wash load. It was the cheapest yet, though. Just $2 to wash and line dry. We strung underwear between the cycle and the tent. Not pretty, but practical.

A YOUNG MAN in lederhosen told us about a hamlet at the end of a "fifteen-mile one-lane-partially-improved-you-can't-really-call-it-a-road place at the edge of the National Park." We headed there almost immediately. The ride had all the obligatory snowy peaks, crashing aqua creeks, and towering evergreens to which we'd grown accustomed. What the man didn't say was that the one-lane road was for two-way traffic and there was a tunnel that had a blind curve in it. You just don't realize how much light comes from the other end of the tunnel until a bend blocks it out.

CHRISTIE WAS FREAKED by the tunnel and I must admit to some worries of my own. She thought it would be better to walk through but I convinced her our odds were better if we got in and out fast, which meant riding.

I'D TRUSTED RICK this far so I reluctantly agreed. Our single headlight beamed into the tunnel. Rick honked all the way through.

IT WAS WORTH a bit of terror. The village was magical. A complete tour took about 15 minutes. A rushing stream, rows of guesthouses (*gasthaus*), and dozens of hikers in proper knee-highs with walking sticks completed what the town had to offer.

Christie screamed her way back through the tunnel so I didn't need to honk.

I COOKED A very American dinner. Pork chops, baked beans, and corn on the cob. The addition of my Italian skillet and Prague platter gave me more options. My galley was stocked with just a one-burner propane stove, one small pot, silverware, two cloth napkins, and a metal bowl and coffee mug each. It wasn't Sur La Table but it served us well.

WE DINED AT the community picnic table, enjoying the company of a couple from Perth, Australia. They planned to visit the United States and wanted to know our favorite places and how to rent a car. Trying to explain America was a challenge and we queried back, knowing that someday we wanted to see Australia. We agreed to email when we all got back home. Of course, we didn't but that's often the nature of travel friendships.

AUGUST 16 Our wonderful neighbors left for a day hike and put their chairs in front of our tent again. Christie delivered a thank you card and a bottle of wine to their tent. And this amazes me. No matter where we are, she comes up with an appropriate gift or card. Makes me wonder what else she's got hiding in her saddle bag.

THE LOANED CHAIRS were a perfect excuse for hanging around the campsite; the sweetness of doing nothing, *la dolce far niente*. Midday we skipped the bus and rode the bike the short distance into the National Park. Our motorcycle gloves came in handy for a snowball fight on the edge of a crystal blue lake.

BACK IN ZERNEZ, I left Christie at the market while I filled the tank and chatted with five Germans on sport bikes. One of the riders had worn out the knee pads on his leathers, reminding me what a rookie I was. We hadn't even come close to leaning over that far. Sparks from the corners of Woody's metal saddle bags wouldn't be the only sparks to fly. Better to ride a bit upright.

The community event that Christie had insisted we attend was a fitting finale for our Zernez stay. We were the only Americans out of 60 or so in attendance. It was the Swiss version of a Chamber of Commerce barbecue. Most of the folks were from our campground and the Mayor made a big deal out of the fact

that Christie was their best promoter. I wasn't surprised but it made for an extra special evening because she knew everyone there.

We shared picnic tables, drank beer, and bellied up to a buffet that resembled the spread at an American Fourth of July. One thing this picnic had that I'd never seen before, though, was the Alphorn.

The Alphorn is the one on postcards that makes you

think "mountains, sheep, and lederhosen." It's eight feet long, made of spruce and since medieval times has been used for sending messages like audible smoke signals from mountain top to mountain top. Demonstrating my willingness to make a fool of myself, I took a turn. It looked fairly straightforward but all I could produce was a weak honk. A tolerant chuckle came from the audience who were probably grateful they hadn't volunteered.

Enjoying a local event was a bonus and the reason we weren't following an itinerary. Of course, having a wife who bothers to translate posters in the marketplace was necessary too.

LEAVING ZERNEZ WAS poignant. We'd gotten into a bit of a routine and made acquaintances beyond "Hello." Riding out of the familiar meadow, I thought, "Will we meet any of these nice folks again? Probably not." But we take a bit of each person with us.

"The journey, not the arrival, matters."

– T.S. ELIOT

CHAPTER 14

PAPER CLIP TURNS

AUGUST 17 It was a diamond of a day. Rode up Julierpass and down the other side, past a large lake and rushing streams. Swiss villages lined the route and we stopped in Flims for lunch.

Until the last decade, Flims dairymen delivered their raw milk to a dairy store in town. The building is, sadly, now a tourist information center and the milk is being treated elsewhere. But the quiet village was traditionally a winter home for the dairymen whose animals grazed on the lush green slopes in summer.

Ski runs crisscrossed the landscape and I found it ironic that we found ourselves at famous ski destinations only in the summer. We're both skiers but we never arranged to go back in the winter. Another perplexity to mull over.

A train track ran the pass route with a cog rail in the center for traction going uphill and braking on the downhill side. We whizzed by a train full of tourists and I felt pretty smug that we were on a motorcycle not a train. My ego couldn't get too big, though, because bicyclists rode the route. Their powerful legs and stamina made me feel like a wimp.

We'd gotten good at moving in harmony at the turns. Ascending Oberlap Pass, I had the thought that the rhythm could get hypnotic but a sign reminded me not to get too comfortable. It was rectangular in shape, with a black drawing of a winged motorcycle. It meant, "Be careful or you'll fly off the cliff and join the angels."

NARROW ROADS AND hairpin turns. Keeping tempo with Rick's upper body was more like a fox trot than a waltz. We shared the road with hay trucks and tourist buses, trains, and bicycles; through tunnels and along that same aqua river. It was a lovely ride with no rain all the way to Andermatt.

But then heaven's faucet opened. It came down in curtains for about 30 minutes, soaking everything. The utter completeness of it made me laugh out loud.

We moved into a *zimmer* that included breakfast and underground parking at a reasonable price. Between rain showers, we explored town and bought a cheap portable radio so we could listen to music in our room. It operated on batteries so we could use it at campgrounds, too. I was thrilled. It was about the same size as four decks of cards and Rick agreed to store it in his saddle bag between pairs of socks. What a guy.

WE VISITED A museum in a 200-year-old house. A photo collection explained early construction of the passes and one whole section was dedicated to a local ski hero, Bernhard Russi, the Olympic gold medal winner in the downhill in Japan and silver medal winner in Innsbruck.

AUGUST 18   Rick was whistling before coffee and cheerfully headed out the door with a wrench in his hand. Usually he muttered and groaned when the motorcycle required him to lie on the ground, so I was curious. When he came back to the room carrying both saddle bags, I said, "Uhh, honey, is there something you haven't told me?"

"It's the Alps!" he said with the expression of a teenager in love.

"Yeah, it's been the Alps for a while so what's different today?"

He gave me one of those, "I guess girls just don't get it" looks and didn't say a word.

I DIDN'T WANT Christie to know we might need knee pads for today's ride. With the bags stored in the room we weren't just lighter but we'd be able to lean harder into the turns without scraping the metal corners on the pavement.

The day started easy. Gotthard Pass was long, narrow and cobblestone with a red brick centerline. Perfect on a motorcycle.

Dropping into Airolo, I was surprised at the presence of a military base with troops and military vehicles, shrines, and memorials. History says that the place had Roman tombs from the second and third centuries. The ruins of a castle are thought to be from a 13th-century noble family. All very interesting but it was riding Alp passes that had my attention so we rode on.

WITHOUT THE REAR bag to lean on and side bags for arm rests, I'd lost my cocoon. I wrapped my arms tightly around Rick for what I guessed would be a long day with shorter stops. This would be our only day to ride passes without saddle bags and being a boy Rick just couldn't wipe the silly grin off his face. I was less thrilled but this wasn't my day so I kept quiet.

HEADING UP THE Nufenenpass, rushing streams ran parallel to the winding road and I kicked up the speed. At the summit, a magnificent border of glaciers and snowy peaks framed the view of the green valley far below. Christie said the roads bent like paper clips and I had to agree.

RIDING THE SWITCHBACKS early in the morning, we were alone, unless the magnificence of the mountains and crashing creeks could be counted as company. As the sun rose higher in the sky, the number of bikers grew, congregating as skiers do at the tops and bottoms of good runs to gaze and to share stories.

Rick marked the map on his tank bag with notes from the other riders about their favorite passes. Apparently, there was a difference and some were "more fun than others." The day had taken on the energy of a fraternity party. Rick thought it was fun but more than once it got a little too exciting and I screamed and picked up my feet when the pedals scraped the pavement, sending up sparks.

At every summit there was a gift shop and we gave great thought to which sticker to buy. It was always a little ceremony when we added a sticker to our growing collection. While Rick carefully placed the newest addition, I wandered across the street. Cow bells chimed and the spray of a waterfall misted into a rainbow. I would have loved to trade my long pants, heavy boots, and leather jacket for sandals and shorts but there were more ribbons of roads that Rick was antsy to ride. I reluctantly climbed back on.

WE DESCENDED INTO Ulrichen and up to Gletsch. The phrase, "The road is the reason," came to mind. At the top of Grimselpass, a metal sculpture of two bikers greeted us. Every shop had a "welcome bikers" banner waving. On this day, wearing leathers and carrying helmets was common instead of an oddity.

BOTH GRIMSELPASS AND Furkapass had broader turns and wider roads. It was like skiing long traverses instead of the stem turns we'd been making. Of course, that meant Rick could go faster. The blur on my left was a dark green forest and the scribble of a stream stayed with us on the right. We flew between the two, rocketing downhill.

I WAS IN cycle heaven but Christie tapped my shoulder indicating that a stop was in order. She'd seen a sign about an ice cave that we were apparently going to check out.

WITH OUR HELMETS slung over our arms, we paid the entry fee and headed inside Rhone Glacier. It was only about two hundred yards deep but walking the length of two football fields in an aquamarine tunnel was eerie. Our voices echoed and our breath rose in puffs of cold vapor.

THIS ICE WASN'T anything like ice cubes. It was blue. Because the cave ice was densely packed, it absorbed all the visible light, except the short blue spectrum. Now I knew where the name "ice blue" originated. A character in a polar bear suit wanted to take our pictures but we snapped photos of each other with our own camera instead.

MID-AFTERNOON, NEAR THE town of Realp, I spied a patch of green that was smoother than what we'd been seeing. There, straddling the base of the mountainside, was what looked like a golf course. "Whoa, check it out!" I called.

I SLOWED DOWN and after a few more turns, I saw it, too. "Good eye, mate," I said, nodding and laughing. After a few more turns, I pulled to a stop right next to the tee box.

The pro was a pleasant chap from England who loaned us clubs. He said we should pay for just nine and when we were finished, if we wanted to do another, it would be on the house. Sounded good to me.

There were some very fit looking women playing in front of us. Being a guy, my first instinct was that play might be slow but the hardy lassies scaled the hills like mountain goats and left us far behind. The fairways resembled intermediate ski runs instead of golf holes and there were quite a few where I would have welcomed a ski lift to get to the next tee. Nine holes was all we could handle.

The course was designed by Olympic champion skier, Bernhard Russi, also the club's president. Franz Klammer, another Olympian who dominated the downhill for four consecutive World Cup seasons, was the current club champion. Having the cardio fitness of an Olympian would certainly have helped.

AUGUST 19 I re-attached the saddle bags and we said good bye to our 80-year-old innkeeper. Before he let us leave, he showed us framed pictures of himself as a young ski jumper, ski instructor, and racer. A charming chap.

Just a few miles out of Andermatt were more paper-clip turns. Sometimes Christie called them "pasta paths," or "Z roads," depending on her mood. I just called them "fabulous fun."

Sustenpass was sharp turns, pointy trees, waterfalls, and rivers. I was almost giddy. On some of the passes, I considered riding back down just "cuz" but resisted the temptation.

WITH A LOADED bike, my arms rested comfortably on the bags and I leaned back, thinking it was more like a Lexus than yesterday's Indy ride.

Lichen-spotted green rocks sparkled in the sun. Horizontal meadows stretched far below. Waterfalls dribbled and dashed, crashed and sprayed. They were too plentiful to count and too delightful to ignore. Tunnels came in a series and every time we popped out I gasped at the enormity of the snow-capped mountains in front of us. The pointy tips of ancient trees grabbed at the clouds and stretched the white threads across their fir needles. The views were the most jaw-dropping yet.

In Lauterbrunnen, Rick negotiated city traffic while I watched the Swiss "red cross" flag snap in the wind. Geranium-laden flower boxes lined every window sill. Of course.

AT TOURIST INFORMATION we checked email. At $12 an hour we were quick. When Christie was confident that there wasn't any urgent family news, we followed TI directions to a campground.

A camping cabin was just $8 a day more than pitching the tent so we took it. It was a room I could stand up in complete with four bunk beds and a shelf. We emptied the contents of the saddle bags onto the empty bunks.

THE SUN WAS shining so we took a "vacation" for the rest of the day. We'd already decided that what we were on wasn't a "vacation." We hadn't agreed on whether it was an adventure, a project, or insanity but whatever it was, we sometimes needed a vacation from it. Wearing sandals and shorts, we found chairs and relaxed into them.

AUSSIE, CANADIAN, KIWI, and a few Mexican and Korean teens were camped in a group nearby. They were on a 47-day tour. We chatted and felt like missionaries for the American lifestyle. For many of the kids, ours was their first conversation with an American.

AUGUST 20 Motorcycle boots made good hiking shoes so we were ready and the sky was blue. From what we could discern, the bus to the base of the Schilthorn cable car only ran hourly so we headed there on foot.

THAT'S RIGHT. *"THE bus went every hour, so we walked."* It was written in both of our journals. "Why" wasn't explained. We weren't in a hurry so the reason for choosing to walk instead of puttering away 40 minutes had to be chalked up to dual personality disorders.

At 4,500 feet, between Stechelberg and Mürren, is Gimmelwald, the setting of the Swiss children's novel, *Heidi*.

In the story, Heidi's an orphan being raised by her grandfather in a tiny village in the Alps. She meets Peter, a young goatherd who is always hungry until Heidi smuggles hard rolls to him. I'd been joking about Heidi's European breakfast rolls since we left the British Isles.

I tried to skip along the service road at the gait of nine-year-old Heidi but I was in my 50s and wearing heavy hiking boots. My body insisted I slow down but the youthful pace played in my head while we walked through the sleepy burg of about 100 residents. The rock face shot straight up the hill and dropped away at our feet. Gimmelwald clung to the ledge in between. No kid could possibly practice soccer or basketball here, I thought; they'd lose a ball to the town below every few minutes. Good place for tending goats, though.

THE PATHS THROUGH town weren't for cars because there was no way for one to get there. The numbers on the houses apparently weren't addresses but fire codes. I took Christie's picture in front of one just to slow us down. She'd wanted to see this place as long as I'd known her, and a dream of decades just couldn't be over in five minutes.

We climbed on the cable car just outside

town and in Mürren switched cars to continue to the top. At 10,000 feet, we stood in awe.

Schilthorn is the longest aerial cableway in the Alps and the traditional start for the "Inferno," the world's longest downhill ski race. A triathlon by the same name had been held the day before. I couldn't fathom the stamina it would take. "Inferno" was an appropriate moniker.

Scenes from the 1969 James Bond 007 movie *On Her Majesty's Secret Service* were filmed here. From the summit, on a clear day, and this one was darn close, a sign said that 200 mountain peaks were visible. We didn't try to count them but it looked like a reasonable estimate.

IN THE DISTANCE lay the Bernese Alps and Mont Blanc. A couple of long gazes in 360-degree circles, a quick turn through the gift shop with too many 007 trinkets, and we filled our water bottles for the all-day hike down the mountain.

The valley floor looked miles away. We stopped next to a snow bank and Rick drew a heart with our initials in it. Our anniversary is in January, my birthday in November, and it was nowhere near Valentine's Day. He was making points big time.

After more than an hour, we'd dropped enough altitude that the landscape lost its snow cover and turned green. The Eiger, Mönch and Jungfrau, all at more than 13,000 feet, hung in front of us like a canvas on a movie set.

IMAGES OF CLINT Eastwood hanging by a rope in the movie, *The Eiger Sanction,* came to mind. I had no desire to be on the North Face myself. This was close enough.

Small flags dotted the edges of the trail. They were guides for the runners in the triathlon the day before.

CRICKETS SOUNDED LIKE castanets, butterflies danced in pairs, and the ground was a carpet of bell-shaped blue flowers and the tiniest white daisies. At Birg and Mürren we stopped to munch on snacks from our packs but mostly we walked. The trail was rocky but as one hour turned into the next we passed through a forest, under waterfalls, and over streams.

My toes jammed forward in my boots and my knees were sore. But we kept walking, taunted by those darn flags reminding me that mortal folks actually ran up this mountain.

And then I fell. It felt so good to be sitting down that my first thought was to stay there. The shale underfoot had been slippery and I was exhausted. Now I was lying in a dusty heap.

Rick turned around and quickly covered the dozen yards that separated us. "What happened? Are you all right? Are you hurt?"

The answers would have been "I fell. Yes. Not much," but I was too tired and shocked to answer. In silence, Rick helped me up, dusted me off and wrapped his arms around me. We stood there for long minutes and it felt good.

CHRISTIE'S FALL HAD apparently stunned her into silence. A tissue and a little water took care of some minor bloodletting.

We'd been walking for nine hours. My feet were sore in my cycle boots but Christie was in pain, too, so I tried to keep my whining to a minimum. She'd twisted her knee and bruised her butt so it was slow going at the end. She's a tough cookie and didn't complain. We finished the walk to the valley floor in lock-step, with her hands pressed into the small of my back for balance and support.

WE HOBBLED TO our cabin and the idea of a beer, some food, and a good night's sleep was dancing in my head like sugar-plums in *The Night Before Christmas*.

AUGUST 21 We woke up to low clouds and cooler temperatures. I was so glad we'd been at the top of the mountain on a clear day that I could almost ignore that my body felt like I'd been in an accident, again. My tailbone ached and my right knee was swollen.

I popped a pain pill and Rick toted our overloaded laundry bag. At just $3 for both wash and dry cycles, I decided we'd get everything clean whether it needed it or not. While the wash was doing its thing we talked about how to spend the day.

PLAN "A" WAS another assault on the mountain but we discarded that for the obvious reasons of pain and clouds. Plan "B" was to visit Bern, which was only an hour away. But "C" won. It was a short hop to Grindelwald.

WE'D BEEN THERE with our daughters on a 10-day family trip to Europe years earlier. My impression then was that it was charming and delightfully foreign. On this trip, Grindelwald was only slightly charming. It looked touristy and Americanized. I doubted it had changed. I knew I had.

AUGUST 22 Leaving the campground we headed into France. In Chamonix, we stretched our legs and got our glasses repaired again. The town was the site of the first winter Olympic games in 1924 and had become a sprawling ski destination. Being sore from the hike, we made it a short day and stopped in Praz-sur-Arley, near Megève.

Set up the tent in our first French camp for $6.50 a night, the cheapest yet. We walked into town, agreeing to meet back at the tent. Christie turned right to find a haircut and I detoured in search of a good local wine. Found it at $1.75 a liter.

When Christie showed up with a butch cut I told her she looked great. I've been married long enough to know when to keep my mouth shut.

WHILE I WAS gone, Rick had set up two "found" chairs and a round plastic table so I dropped our groceries at waist height instead of on the ground and happily sank into one of the white plastic chairs.

I was charmed by the melodic nature of the language. Rick and I both had a bit of high school French so we could conjure up meaning better than in Gaelic or German.

I wrote in my journal. *"The bathrooms are coed. The flush has a hose into the toilet bowl and the ladies' potty requires standing up to straddle a hole (merci non!) and never forget to BYO paper. O mon dieu!"* Despite the lack of easy toilets, I was happy. I was in France.

OUR LONG-HAIRED NEIGHBOR, Marcel, and his visiting friend, Jerome, a liquor distributor, decided to share our table. Jerome laid out his

"sample kit" of wines and local liqueurs and tried his best to empty the bottles into the three of us. The guys were about our daughter's ages and we didn't have a common language but somehow it didn't matter.

AUGUST 23   The first thing I noticed in the morning was that it was dry. The ground. The tent fly. For the first time since the trip began. The second was that our little table looked like we'd hosted a party for at least a dozen instead of just ourselves and our two neighbors.

We moved the empties and spread out a breakfast picnic. Our camp pals sat down like family and we continued where we'd left off the night before, using a combination of French, English, and some Spanish in an effort to communicate. Mostly we smiled and gestured at each other. I was glad I'd over-bought in the market because Jerome and Marc made themselves right at home with the provisions.

ROLLING UP THE tent and putting away the bed rolls was so much easier when everything was dry.

Jerome had given me some tips on a scenic ride over the Col des Aravis, a mountain pass in the French Alps that connects La Clusaz in Haute-Savoie with La Giettaz in Savoie. We rode it before detouring into La Clusaz, a renowned ski town with condos stacked in tiers up the slopes. We passed a ski shop named for a 1960s ski hero of mine, Guy Perillat. I was tempted to stop but afraid I'd also be tempted to spend money.

The curves tossed us back and forth in perfect rhythm. When a Peugeot sedan was hot on my tail, I went even faster, getting into the moment of being one with the big bike.

The road to Flumet had long flowing turns and I was sorry when it was over. On through Albertville, we turned toward Moûtiers, looking for a short cut on back roads. Route D94 to Celliers looked like the answer. It was narrow and bumpy but wound higher into the French Alps, ending at the Col de la Madeleine.

That was where I first saw writing on the road. It was either chalk or a washable paint. Product advertisements and directional arrows had turned the pavement into colorful billboards. We'd been out of touch with the news and hadn't realized that the Tour de France had ridden these roads. Knowing it now connected the dots and explained the increase in bicycle traffic, too. Locals were inspired by the big race and some even passed us on the narrow descent into St. Michel de Maurienne.

Turning onto D902 to Valloire I kicked up the speed. The ascent at Col du Galibier was fast with no guard rails. We'd done four passes in Austria, three in the Italian Dolomites, seven in Switzerland, and this was our second in France. Ahhh.

In Embrun, we set up camp near a lake where swarms of European tourists lay in the sun. The family-style camping resort was $10 a night and a lakeside patio sold beer for $1.50. All around the lake were scruffy vacation amenities including boat rental, putt-putt golf, and restaurants. We got busy having fun.

My IMPRESSION WAS that here, more than other places we'd been, people played. They were on rafts in the rivers, on horseback in the fields, and sipping wine at road-side tables. They looked contented, which was apparently contagious.

Lounging on the pebbly beach under a faded blue sky, Rick took sidelong glances at the topless ladies when he thought my eyes were closed. Feeling very French, I joined them. Isn't there a saying, "When in France do as the French do?" Maybe not, but there should be.

AUGUST 24   Breakfast was a baguette because dining on anything else would be so "un-French." The long sticks of bread with their paper-wrap handles were as common as cardboard coffee cups in the U.S. We sat on a park bench with the long loaf between us. We broke it into chunks, finding it crusty on the outside, soft and doughy on the inside. Crumbs fell to the ground and tiny birds retrieved them almost before they landed. Very lucky birds.

RODE TO SAINT-CLEMENT-SUR-DURANCE to see Fort Vauban, an imposing building of stone with commanding views of two valleys below. It was used as a military school for young officer candidates. The Fortifications of Vauban are a series of twelve groups of buildings that form a defensive ring around France. This was the only one we saw but I loved that it was constructed by Sébastien Le Prestre de Vauban in the 1600s for King Louis XIV. America just doesn't know about "old."

The road wound up the hill to Vars, elevation 6,000 feet, where photos in *Ski Magazine* had featured images of sleek body suits and aerodynamic helmets racing at speeds over 100 mph. No thanks. I'd take Woody up to 100 but not skis.

IDENTICAL TOWNS WITH more ski lifts. We stopped in one for a picnic and a walk. The houses were faded yellow plaster festooned with sagging shutters. No more bright red flowers in window boxes. It was sloppy compared to Switzerland but with a charm of its own. It was a lazy ride back to the campground under a dusty blue sky.

WE TOOK OUR sleeping mats down to the water to soak up some sun and people watch. My "people" turned out to be a tall redhead with shapely legs, flat stomach, topless, of course. Did I mention that I love France?

"The world is a canvas."

– THOREAU

CHAPTER 15

VAN GOGH, VERNAZZA, VECCHIO

AUGUST 25 We got an early start, packing quietly so we wouldn't disturb our sleeping neighbors. The horizon glowed like the inside of a seashell. I asked Rick to ride slowly so I could watch the beams of light ripple into the high clouds. When I'd had my fill, I told him it was okay to speed up.

WITH NO BREAKFAST, we stopped for an early lunch at a *boulangerie* next to a fig orchard. The shop was stocked with an unprecedented selection of breads, meats, and cheeses and we couldn't resist the smell of fresh baguettes. We joined a couple from Italy under an olive tree to enjoy the spread.

IT WAS LATE August in Provence. We rode slowly behind a tractor until Rick could pass. The land on both sides was dotted with the big earth movers churning over clods of heavy earth while sheep grazed. Huts huddled in the valley, their slate roofs gleaming in the noon sun. Fields of wild thyme alternated with acres of droopy sunflowers. I could imagine the wilted flowers as they'd been a few weeks earlier, full dinner-plate size. The lavender was fading, too, but combined with the thyme, the aroma turned the air into a sachet.

The sun poured itself over us. Summer was nearly done but this was the first time I was sweating under my leathers. We passed a familiar-looking bridge and I did a double-take. It was the one in the Van Gogh painting! I swiveled as far as I dared on the back seat of the bike.

In Arles, I parked in an enclosed garage and we moved into the Hôtel du Musée for two nights. The room had a double bed, real pillows, and air conditioning. I figured that after a quick shower, change to clean shorts and sandals, a few minutes of BBC or CNN on TV, and I'd be ready to explore the Roman walled town.

I knew from the map that Arles was on the Rhône River and linked to the Mediterranean by a canal. And it's where Van Gogh lived. While Rick explored the television possibilities, I went downstairs to check out the hotel grounds.

Through the breakfast room, I found a door to the hotel's backyard and stepped over the sill into a picture book. A long, sheltered lawn was boxed in by tall thick hedges. Primroses lined the edges of the damp grass. Pale, delicate blossoms clung to thin green stems. The air smelled of sweet oranges. A man in a straw hat leaned his rake against a wooden seat and waved for to me to join him. When I got to where he was standing, he handed me a clump of sweet-smelling violets. "Ah, merci beaucoup," I said and patted his arm.

Christie came into the room all smiles and talking about a garden from a fairy tale. She used my coffee cup as a vase and it didn't take a brain surgeon to figure out she was ready to explore.

We walked down cobbled alleyways, barely a lane wide. Near an AD 80 amphitheater, baths and crypts, I went into a shop and bought a Langloise knife with a wine opener. It felt good in my hand and I knew I'd use it a lot even though we only had a month to go.

AUGUST 26   The brochure I picked up said that in the late 1880s Van Gogh left "the cold, grey weather in Paris, following the sun to the south of France." He chose Arles because "the light and warmth were an opportunity to explore color." Looking around, I understood his sentiment.

Van Gogh rented a home he called the "Yellow House" to serve as a "Studio of the South" and he invited Gauguin to join him. We stood on the sidewalk in front of it. I said, "I must be happier than they were. Wasn't it just a couple of months later that Van Gogh got violent?"

"That's what this says," Rick said, focused on the folder in his hand. "They were disagreeing and that led to Van Gogh threatening Gauguin with a razor and cutting off part of his own ear."

"Keep that new knife in your pocket, please," I joked, holding my hand to my ear.

We walked to the hospital where Vincent went increasingly insane. The gardens were immense. A gauzy gold light shafted across the flowers and the light shimmered.

EVEN I COULD see what Christie meant by the "light that enthralls artists." I was almost ready to rent an apartment and stay. Or take up painting.

We stopped at a sidewalk café just to rest but I could have taken up residence for the pastry alone. The croissant was frosted in decadent dark chocolate. I licked my fingers and Christie used hers like little magnets to collect the flakes that fell on the napkin. The thick black coffee was in a cup too small for my fingers and refills were, of course, unthinkable. Christie savored the last sip of hot brew while I found more chocolate to lick off my fingers.

An upcoming bullfight was being promoted on posters throughout Arles. With Christie's acumen for determining our itinerary by translating handbills, I thought maybe we'd be staying. We'd seen a bullfight in Mexico and she told me we weren't going to do it again, which was okay with me.

We walked through a *cryptoporticus*, a covered passageway from 20 BC. It was cool and drippy, a semi-subterranean hallway with vaulted structures above ground that flowed into graceful arches.

Christie was buying our picnic dinner fixings when I nearly collided with an enormous pan of paella. It was at least three feet across with steam rising. Yellow saffron rice filled the edges but sticking out I could see mussels, shrimp tails, white fish, dotted with what Christie said was probably paprika. It looked like heaven but it would take a crowd to do the meal justice.

I BREATHED DEEPLY. Mounds of dark red and rust colored powders were piled two feet high. The air smelled of olives, curry, and lavender. Garlic, cinnamon and cloves. When I finished shopping, Rick carried the jug of wine in his arms and a bag of fruit and cheeses swung at his side. I cradled a whole cooked chicken and we took the load up to our room.

Later that evening, we headed down to the breakfast room, laden with food and plates, but the woman behind the desk hoisted herself to her feet, shook her head and waggled a fist, letting us know without words that our picnic would be elsewhere.

The French have rules that aren't apparent to those passing through. A few days earlier we'd been told not to walk on the grass and another time, not to sit on a curb so I shouldn't have been surprised. We ate on a bench across the street, using our camp coffee mugs as wine glasses and Rick's handy new knife to open the wine and part the chicken.

AUGUST 27 It wasn't the scenic route but the toll roads had speed on their side. Christie doled out $30 for the day. We passed signs for places we'd seen on a previous visit so we didn't need to stop. St. Tropez, Antibes, Cannes, Nice. I exited in Monaco for an overpriced sandwich and diet Coke but added a classy sticker to the saddlebag collection.

All day on the autostrada the Med was in view, except through miles and miles of tunnels. I knew we were back in Italy when the drivers began passing without changing lanes. At 80 mph they just took half ours and kept on going.

THE SKY WAS shockingly blue and the sea reflected it back, blanketing the steep hillside in dancing light. Rick had no chance to even glance; he was busy playing road roulette with the Italian drivers. He had to take my word for it that the hills put on an Aurora Borealis show.

WE GOT LOST in Genoa but finally found our way to Sestri. Long lines of traffic waited to enter a one-lane tunnel leading to the beach. Moped and motorcycle riders wore shorts or silk pants, sandals or leather slippers. No heavy boots or knee pads here.

THE TENTS WERE practically touching each other and the ground was hard as concrete but we were surrounded by a dramatic landscape of sea and mountains. Colorful umbrellas crowded the beach. It was easy to find a rock for Rick to use on the tent stakes because the beach wasn't sand, it was a swirl of rocks. Green, yellow and white with purple pin stripes. I wanted to start a collection but Rick, not too subtly, reminded me that a bag of rocks was not good motor-cycle cargo.

I FINISHED POUNDING the tent stakes and stood to wipe the sweat off when a man came at me, waving his arms and talking fast. He was Italian, our neighbor, and apparently I'd done something wrong. We deciphered that we'd pitched the tent an inch or two over some imaginary line. Not being able, or particularly motivated, to argue in a foreign language, I shoved the tent just a bit, bending the stakes slightly. I smiled with a gesture that was meant to say, "Sorry, is that better?" He gave a curt nod that it was okay now. Or, at least, I thought that's what he meant.

WE WALKED THROUGH Sestri's 12th-century Gualino Castle and a handful of churches. We were killing time until the restaurants opened at 7:30 and we wanted to check the morning train schedule to the Cinque Terre. It seemed that tickets went on sale in a café just before the train left, which was approximately hourly.

MEN PLAYED BOULE on sand courts. Palm-sized lead balls were thrown at a target, like horseshoes. It looked like a serious affair with lots of adult yelling.

At 7:30, a pizzeria owned by a guy named Steve-from-New-Joisey opened. A fine pizza, a few beers, and we were ready to crawl into the tent. But at 10:00 p.m. the promenade was brightly lit. Young and old strolled, sang, and talked. It might as well have been noon. And it was warm. It was the first night we didn't need sleeping bags.

AUGUST 28   The shower had two choices. Cold with a door and a bidet or cold without a door and no bidet. At first, I thought the bidet was a toilet because to the uninitiated it really does look like a toilet with oddly placed water faucets and no flusher.

The shower room had no shelves and no hooks so I held my chamois towel and shower bag in one hand while I tried to wash with the other. European camping had some acrobatic aspects.

WE BOUGHT OUR train tickets where we also downed tiny cups of espresso and hard crusty rolls. Our plan was to ride the train to the southernmost of the five hillside towns and spend the day walking back, along the path above the Med, through the Cinque Terre.

WRAPPED IN THE blue skirt of the sea were Riomaggiore, Manarola, Corniglia, Vernazza, Monterosso. I rolled the names off my tongue, enjoying the feel. Bell towers chimed the hour as the train pulled out of the station.

Via Colombo is Riomaggiore's main street and we walked its length. Twice. Anchovy skiffs lay upturned in the cobbled streets. *Alimentari* shops peddled strawberries and cherries, an assortment of salami, cheeses and olives. We munched our way through town. Signs indicated history pre-dating AD 500 and still it was charming.

A 45-minute walk took us to Manarola. Swimmers dove off the seawall into the clear blue water. More colorful boats lay with their hulls up along the narrow roadways. Houses climbed the hillsides, stacked on top of each other like crayon boxes left to melt in the sun.

AND OUR CAMERA quit working. Spewing more swear words than I'd heard from her in a decade, Christie disappeared into a small store and came out with a disposable one.

We stopped for a snack of fresh *acciughe* (anchovies) with lemon, olive oil, and crusty bread. Over our stand-up picnic, next to a fat pile of yellow fishing nets, we met Phil and Janet, a dentist and a lawyer from Connecticut on a three-week vacation. We walked with them as far as Corniglia, where they bypassed the steep steps and continued on the trail. They had more to see that day but we took our time.

WE ZIGZAGGED UP a few hundred rough-cut steps to the town. Laundry flapped in the on-shore breeze. Soft-hued buildings were stacked like blocks arranged by a four-year-old. We bought a bottle of chilled white wine for $3. The cork was loose fitting and there was no label on the green bottle. Sitting on stairs facing the Mediterranean, we snacked on prosciutto and fromage between swigs of the crisp wine straight from the bottle.

Leaving Corniglia, the trail was just wide enough for two goats to pass. Vineyards lay in stripes, terracing the hillside below. Above us, young apricot and olive trees poked out of the ground like rows of fat toothpicks.

AS THE SUN rose, so did the trail. In the shade of some olive trees, we met a Canadian girl named Erin. She was two years younger than our youngest daughter and backpacking across Europe. We walked single file and stopped to let others pass.

` "I just love that you two are out here like college students." She looked back and forth at each of us, questioningly, "You know what I mean?"

Christie spoke first. "Well, yes. Our oldest daughter did a college semester in London and then wandered across Europe."

We were familiar with the concept but we weren't trying to be collegiate. Walking in front of me, Christie continued to try to explain our motivation. "We set out to see Europe and chose to do it on a motorcycle for adventure and with camping gear because we're cheap."

Erin laughed and I did, too. Here was my 50-plus-year-old wife with a Master's degree and a Junior League background, wearing dusty motorcycle boots, explaining our atypical choice. I put my arm around her and said, "Erin, are you saying your parents wouldn't choose four months on a motorcycle as a way to see Europe?"

It was her turn to laugh, "Not a chance!" She was still chuckling a hundred yards up the path.

In Vernazza, we bought Erin an ice cream and said goodbye. We explored the fishing village, founded about AD 1000. The town's relative wealth was in evidence; the elegant arches and elaborate doorways seemed out of place. We explored Belforte, a medieval castle built in the mid-1500s to protect the village from pirates, and walked on.

We made quick work of town number five, Monterosso, and caught the train back to the campground in time for dinner and to watch the sun drop into the Med.

DINNER WAS A beach-walk-moveable-feast. We started at the Italian version of a hot dog stand serving bruschetta. A skinny man wearing a T-shirt and wielding a dangerous-looking knife toasted bread on an open fire and brushed it with olive oil. With bare fingers, he rubbed the toast with garlic and topped it with fresh chopped tomatoes and basil broken from a bouquet in his waistband.

I couldn't tell whether it was the fresh olive oil, the beach setting, or his bare hands that made it heavenly. But that was something else I didn't need to decide. After more than a few, we wandered on down the beach and bought a pair of grilled seafood skewers. They were edible souvenirs washed down with wine from our coffee mugs. A square of black dark chocolate before brushing our teeth was a fitting end to the day.

But I was too wired too sleep. Not work-wired or worry-wired, I was in a frenzied high brought on by Mediterranean breezes and colorful villages that clung to their cliffs. Upturned boats in the streets. The music of a language punctuated by energetic gestures. The drama had me higher than inhaling in Amsterdam. I was glad we were taking the next day off; I wanted time to preserve the images and I did that best sitting still.

AUGUST 29   Just yards from the tent, we rented beach chairs and a shade umbrella, creating a day camp on the rocky beach. We were reading *Milagro Beanfield War*. Christie was nearly finished with the front half so I had strict orders to finish so she could continue.

Watching family dynamics with a foreign soundtrack was good entertainment and we witnessed more than a few child tantrums worthy of Academy Awards. Men were actively involved in child care. Most of the ladies were slim, attractive, and fashionably dressed, looking good without clothes, too. I heard zero English spoken.

MY VERSION OF a swimsuit was a camisole and underpants since everything we packed needed to do double duty. We splashed each other in the cool Mediterranean and read.

Midday I headed to town. I needed to replenish an eczema cream that had cost $40 in Arizona, plus the obligatory doctor visit to get the prescription in the first place. I had no idea how I was going to get more in a small Italian beach village but I needed to try. I showed the nearly empty tube to the pharmacist and without a single word, he handed me an identical replacement. For $4.50.

THAT EVENING, WE played cards and enjoyed a couple of beers with our now talkative and laughing neighbor. This was the same guy who'd taken me to task for pitching the tent too close. At midnight, when we parted company, I said to Christie, "Amazing what a couple of inches can do for international relations." She didn't reply but I think she was laughing.

AUGUST 30   I loved waking up with a map of Europe as my day planner. Being with Rick 24/7 made me happy, too. Even riding was mostly okay. But fitting our gear back in the saddlebags had grown tedious. The stuff was like a Chia Pet®, seemingly expanding overnight.

The first order of business on moving day was always to open the air valves on the mats and, while they deflated, to stuff the down sleeping bags into their compression bags. The morning was muggy and the hard ground painful to kneel on. I rolled, stuffed, and shoved the gear. In a bad mood, I knocked my coffee over, soaking the right knee of my jeans.

RICK SNAGGED A finger nail on the bed roll and was bleeding. He held a tissue to it while I searched for a band aid.

"I'm not sure I've got another month's worth of energy for this," he grumbled, abandoning the tissue and sucking the blood off his finger.

I was quiet for a moment, unwrapping the band aid and thinking.

"What if, in Florence, we could find a place to stay where we could leave the camping gear? We'd see Tuscany, do the hill towns, and stay in hotels without all this gear. Would that help?"

I BENT TO kiss the fingers that were securing the band aid. "Brilliant," I smiled. "We'd have to go back to Florence to collect the gear but I could see *David* twice!"

In a more cheerful mood, I shoved the tent in its stuff sack and thanked the angels in charge of spouse assignments. Next, I beat the Thermarests® into submission. One at a time, I kneeled on them, squeezing and rolling them tight enough to slide into their waterproof bags before bungeeing them to the top of the saddle bags.

It was a fast trip on the autostrada with a short stop and walk in the walled city of Lucca. The walls are a pedestrian promenade that circles the town and that was perfect for us. I could keep an eye on our loaded bike and we could stretch our legs at the same time.

Entering Florence (Firenze), scooter madness took over and I played my "when in Rome" card even though we were in Florence. Riding on the shoulder or in the oncoming lanes looked like standard operating procedure. I drew the line at riding on the sidewalks.

I INQUIRED AT three hotels with no luck. They were either full, too expensive, or no one spoke enough English for me to be able to convey that we wanted to leave a large pile of gear that we would return to collect on an uncertain date. I was getting discouraged when Rick suggested we try the Tourist Information office at the train station.

I stood in a second formidable line. The first had been for train tickets, not hotel reservations. Long before I got to the front, a very pleasant looking man handed me a brochure. He and his wife ran Cristina's Family House. He told me the price and said that his wife spoke some English. "Eureka!" Gestures were enough to communicate that I wanted him to follow me to the bike. I wanted him see the gear we would store, on the off-chance he understood my request.

I SAT ASTRIDE, in front of the Florence train station, wondering what was taking so long when I saw her headed my way. At last. I fired Woody up and expected her to climb on. Instead, she just stood there. That's when I noticed the attractive man standing beside her. He couldn't be a hitchhiker, not on a motorcycle. And if he'd been flirting with my wife and they were going to run away together, they certainly wouldn't be standing here in front of me.

Her voice broke me out of the crazy reverie.

"Good news, honey, this nice man and his wife, Cristina, have a B & B that might be our answer."

"Awesome," I said climbing off. I took off one glove and we shook hands, followed by a few words that couldn't be called a conversation but were a pleasant attempt.

Christie held the brochure on my back opened to the map. While I drove she called out instructions the likes of: "Left – oh, back there – go around the block." "No not here." "Now right, damn. One way," and somehow we arrived at Cristina's.

Our room was on the second floor and comfortable enough. We didn't dwell on the room's details. We were in Florence, home of Michelangelo's *David*. I'd wanted to see it nearly as long as Christie had dreamed of going to Heidi's alpine village.

The original was carved in the early 1500s and it came to symbolize the defense of civil liberties in the Florentine Republic. We walked quickly but I really picked up the pace as we got closer. Suddenly he was right in front of me. Or I was in front of him.

David. A masterfully chiseled slim, nude male three times my height. He looked victorious yet at peace; a vision of young male perfection. I moved slowly, 360 degrees. Twice. I felt tears and was only slightly embarrassed. Wiping them away with the back of my hand, I stood completely still and stared.

The statue was moved to the Accademia Gallery in Florence in 1873 and I was standing within a few feet of it. Being here was worth the whole trip and I could see that Christie was moved as well. We walked away but *David* called me back until, on the third try, I let myself move on to see Florence.

BATHED IN THE glow of a Tuscany sunset, the Arno River looked like molten gold. With a 14-carat river flowing below us, it seemed appropriate that the Ponte Vecchio bridge was lined with jewelry stores. Centuries ago the buildings were butcher shops, which was okay with me because from one angle, the Arno glowed blood red.

A long walk took us through churches and past more statuary. We stopped under an awning; color choices gleamed from the freezer case. Lemon, jasmine, watermelon, kiwi. I ordered my gelato in a cone, Rick preferred a cup. After that, we stopped for *sorbetti* more often than our motorcycle pants could comfortably handle.

When it was time to go home we realized we were thoroughly lost. But Rick has a great sense of direction so we kept walking until he figured it out.

AUGUST 31 We explored museums and palaces, followed by more museums, paintings, and statues. Rick's the one with the art training so I just stayed close so we wouldn't get separated and mostly people watched. In the piazza, pale stone buildings crowded together. The aroma of fresh sausage and just-picked herbs collided in a delightful way. Following a limestone brick alleyway, we found the Uffizi Gallery.

THE LINE AT the Uffizi stretched to infinity so we went to the Palazzo Vecchio instead. I'm a huge fan of the Medici period and walking through their quarters and standing on the dais of the Italian Parliament made me think of da Vinci and Michelangelo standing in the same spot, competing for a new art project. Ceilings were painted in the ornate style of the 15th century and the view from the windows of the Tuscan capitol looked like one of Hermann's postcards.

We returned to our room to wait out a thunderstorm and read a purloined copy of *USA Today*. At 5:30 we returned to the Uffizi and voilà, no lines. Paintings by Bottticelli, Michelangelo, Raphael, and da Vinci lined the walls and I was overcome.

At a deli-style cantina we got another lesson in Italian culture. I figured that the signs next to each sandwich in the case showed what they cost. Seemed logical, so we chose what we wanted and asked for it "to go." *"Per andare, per favore."*

The man in a white starched coat waved that we should "Take a seeet." It seemed rude to decline. I asked if the price was the same whether we sat or took it "to go," using appropriate gesture and speaking clearly. It seemed like he said "no difference." It was pouring outside and the man was so gracious and enthusiastic that we sat down.

When the bill came my guess had been right. Sitting down had doubled the price and I went psycho-ugly-American. It just riled my bones to be so blatantly taken advantage of. I shouted, waved my arms, and generally ruined the meal for everyone in the place. A sorry experience. I tossed down some cash, the portion of the bill I thought I owed, and left, probably letting the door slam like a true American.

A BIT DAMAGED by the price gouging and Rick's over-the-top reaction, we splashed across Florence, through puddles, staying under awnings and detouring through buildings wherever possible.

At an internet café, we learned that our son-in-law would be in Paris on business, could we see him? Sadly, no. Not only couldn't we get there but in our four-month trip we skipped both Paris and Venice completely. A quarter of a year is a long trip but not long enough to see everything.

An email from a boating friend suggested that we meet at her mom's house in the south of France, and that did match our schedule. We hadn't seen Sylvette in over a year so we had lots of stories to share and I replied with an enthusiastic, "We'll be there" and a range of probable arrival dates.

In another match-up request, our daughter's Italian friend, Grazia, was heading toward Florence and could meet us there when we returned.

We left the internet café with a couple of somewhat specific plans on the horizon. A first.

"The world is a book and those who do not travel read only a page"

– ST. AUGUSTINE

CHAPTER 16

ALL ROADS LEAD TO ROME

SEPTEMBER 1   Leaving Florence, an early morning yellow light bathed the wide cobbled streets, spreading a buttery glow on the famous statuary. Or maybe my delight was fueled by the fact that we'd left the camping gear at Cristina's. Our hosts had been a little uncomfortable with the idea that we didn't know exactly when we'd be back so Rick had picked a date and made a reservation to appease them.

WOODY FELT LIGHT with only the fixed saddle bags and no extra bundles strapped to their tops. We were headed for Tuscan and Umbrian hill towns. We'd stay in hotels or inns.

First stop was San Gimignano, easy to spot from a distance with a dozen medieval towers making an intriguing silhouette. With our helmets and jackets locked to the bike, we walked the narrow streets and stopped at shops selling leather goods, colorful tiles, and clothing. Christie bought a red leather purse for our daughter, Lisa. The pocket she thought was for a cell phone was actually for cigarettes but coming from a culture of non-smokers, it didn't occur to her until we got home.

Some high-quality leather book covers caught my eye. The only reason I didn't take a half dozen home was that to pack them I'd need to empty a third of Christie's saddlebag and that wouldn't have gone over well.

A HARPIST WAS entertaining on a plaza. Italians sat on hard chairs, sipping from tiny cups, and we stood next to the wall of a Roman villa to listen. It was lovely until the music screeched and stopped. A Japanese tourist had stuck her head between the man and his instrument. Apparently, she was posing for her friend to take a photo. The musician wasted no time untangling himself and sprinting from the courtyard. Or, at least, he ran as fast as a short man carrying a harp can scuttle.

When I stopped being horrified, I started laughing. "Can you believe the chutzpah it takes to do that?"

"Well, yeah, I can. Remember, I lived in Japan. They'll do anything for a photo." Rick was laughing too.

WE CLIMBED THE stairs of a church and just inside the thick doors was a row of baskets, spilling over with bright colored shawls and piles of skirts. The selection was for female tourists who came wearing inappropriate church attire. I suspected that American women were most likely to need the coverings. One advantage of riding a motorcycle, Christie was always covered up.

Further south, Christie had a view of plowed fields, yellow and red villas, and farmhouses with red tile roofs while I kept my eyes on the narrow road. She "oohed and aahhed" and I stopped when she said, "Honey, I need to touch those grapes." Her love affair with grapes was beginning to resemble the reverence ladies in churches showed when they fingered their rosaries.

Rick is such a sweetie. My request was crazy but he stopped the bike on a narrow shoulder and I climbed off, scrambling down a small dirt bank and into the vineyard. I shaded my eyes and looked out on parallel rows of grapes zippering up the hills. The grapes clustered in perfect pyramids, as if someone had used a pool rack to align them. Sunlight slipped through in beams and ripples; liquid silver dappled their purple skins. The grand globes basked in the sunshine, seeming to ripen as I watched.

Rick patiently waited while I crouched in the dirt and breathed in their sweetness. The dusty bundle even smelled purple. "They're just begging to be wine," I said. Climbing back on, I cradled a purloined cluster in my lap.

After the vineyards, I was treated to fields of droopy, dry-headed sunflowers. Next came cornfields. Then pumpkins and squash. Every few minutes the painting changed.

In Siena, we locked and covered our jackets and helmets and walked down narrow streets, past Gothic palaces and aristocratic mansions with medieval gates to one of Europe's oldest universities, founded in 1240.

The Duomo was built in the early 1200s, too, but we'd been in Europe so long it didn't seem terribly old anymore. I'd read that Siena is known for its wine but also for a unique marble. I planned to experience both and the second was right there in front of us. The facade of the church was a rich orange with exposed purple and black veins.

We sat on the edge of the Fonte Gaia and looked skyward, admiring an assortment of medieval palaces. On the fan-shaped main square, we explored a 14th-century chapel. But the highlight was taking a seat in the historic Piazza del Campo, even though it was empty with the *palio* still five days away.

Part historical pageant and part horse race, the *Palio delle Contrade* has been held since the 15th century. Competitors show their colors, parade in the streets, and party. On the big day, the horses gallop three times around the track. That's it. Even though the Piazza is large, "It wouldn't take long," I said to Christie.

"Yeah, just a blur and the race would be over," she said.

FROM THE FIFTH row of the nearly empty arena, I imagined costumed jockeys riding bareback. Event lore says that there are kidnappings of the most skilled jockeys and bribery is common. Horses get skewered by the guardrails and when a similar fate meets a jockey, a riderless horse might win. Despite the colorful costumes and medieval energy, it sounded like mayhem.

THE HOTEL ROOMS we checked on confirmed our decision to move on. They were uninteresting and while we were sure that Siena was worth more time than we gave it, after a few hours, we left.

Riding southeast through Tuscany and into drier Umbria we were headed for Cortona, the setting for Frances Mayes' 1996 book, *Under the Tuscan Sun*. Being a writer, Christie was intrigued.

THE LADY AT the hotel desk wore a crocheted shawl around slim shoulders. She led us up flight after flight of stairs, stopping only when the stairs ended. Our home under the eaves had two rooms, one looking over the street. I looked at the motorcycle on the cobbled street below. It looked tiny enough to put in a Christmas stocking. The other room had a view of the hills beyond town. You'd need to be three feet tall to walk the perimeter but it was charming.

I THOUGHT ABOUT wearing my helmet so I wouldn't bang my head but Christie agreed to take the bed nearest the short wall. I fell asleep quickly for a needed nap.

I SIPPED SHERRY and our little radio played softly. I gazed out the window and decided that Frances Mayes' *Bramasole* was the house in my view. When my glass was empty, I took a walk.

The streets were quiet except for an occasional burst of household chatter from an open window. I looked up at one of my favorite sights, laundry flapping in the breeze. Dark blue leg shapes and white rectangles snapped and waved while sherbet tones of smaller items ruffled gently.

After an hour, I returned to the room and Rick was awake. We headed out to walk the Etruscan portion of the city wall. The landscape fell away and disappeared down a hill bathed in pink and yellow. We turned around and headed back to town to see what restaurant might appeal for dinner.

A SIGN WITH a non-Italian, Etruscan or Gothic name caught my eye. "*Southwest Café - Route 66,*" it announced in bright red letters. It even had the iconic shape on the "66." We looked over the menu. Pasta was $6-7 and a side of meat for about $8. Sounded good so we went in.

After dinner we had some bad news. Sitting at a table was an extra $4. Water was $2. The meat was priced per hectogram so the size we'd gotten was $26 for a greasy, grey, tough slab of shoe leather we hadn't eaten. The bill had grown to $45.

I attempted to discuss the disparity with the waitress but I spoke English and she Italian. She looked at me with eyes like martini olives. They were beautiful but they didn't blink. It was unnerving so I asked for the owner or manager.

"Three hours," she said, still staring.

We weren't going to wait but we couldn't very well ask for change when we planned to pay just part of the bill so off Christie went, into the dark streets, in search of small bills. When she returned, I paid what I thought was fair, a compromise at $30, included a nice tip, and left the name of our hotel if they wanted to talk about it.

"Is it a national Italian pastime to screw the customer?" I muttered, hurrying toward our hotel.

"It seems like it. But they don't get too worked up in the process," Christie said.

"Yeah, that's true, but they've sure mastered the fine art of getting into your pocket without your permission." I fully expected to see flashing lights of "la Policia" at any moment.

"I wonder if they do it to their countrymen, too, or if it's just for foreigners?" Christie asked.

"Good question. Let's ask Grazia when we see her," I said. "In the meantime if we're gonna avoid this grief, we'll have to rely on self-serve-stand-up dining till we get into France."

Climbing the flights to our room, Christie laughed, "Or skip dinner. We're outgrowing our leathers."

SEPTEMBER 2 Leaving town at first light, I think Christie was looking over her shoulder for the gendarmes and not Frances Mayes.

WE DIDN'T NEED maps or directions because hill towns were easy to find. They're the ones on the tops of the hills. It was almost too easy.

Where bus tours converged, we didn't stay long. To avoid the crowds in Assisi, we wandered a back alley of cobbled lanes. Inside the basilica of St. Frances we watched the devout, gazed at the statuary, and rode on.

AT TODI, WE were charmed. "I can sure understand the pull for ex-pats to live in one of these towns," I said to Christie.

"Yeah, they're large enough to have a community of English speakers," she replied, with a faraway look.

I knew I didn't need to ask what she was thinking. I just needed to wait a minute and I'd hear all about it.

"There's a lot to love about Italy," she said after just a few beats. "There's laughter in the language and these hill towns are stages for a fairy tale. But when foreigners move here I think they fix up run-down farmhouses and that's not our strong suit."

Our first home together had been a fifty-plus-year-old gracious and stately home in Portland, Oregon, but it had needed more handyman skills than I had in my tool box. We'd sold rather quickly and hadn't looked back. Todi was like that. We loved it and moved on.

In Orvieto, we chose a modern hotel in the lower part of town. It had a lobby with tables where we could play cards and eat our picnic dinner (some things about Italy were more user friendly than in France), and the room had air conditioning, a television, and a balcony where we could hang laundry. With breakfast included, we sealed the deal.

It was easier to ride without the camping gear but navigating foreign streets and seeing new sights took everything out of me. We booked two nights.

ORVIETO'S STREETS WERE flat and easy to walk. Honeycombed with Etruscan caves and an ancient olive press, there was something interesting around every corner. The town was very much alive but with a past dating before the Etruscans, to 800 BC. A line of women trudged by, carrying canvas bags of fresh fruit, vegetables, and bread. Two younger gals pushed strollers so huge they could never flatten to fit in a car so I was sure they did all their errands on foot. And little children splashed in a fountain. It was just people going about their daily routines but in a manner we'd never see in America.

SEPTEMBER 3 The Duomo glowed like a jewel against a cloud-puffed sky. On a bench facing the grand church, three men sat reading papers, halos of pipe smoke circling above their heads.

Across the street, housed in a former palace, was what turned out to be my favorite museum, *Museo Claudio Faina*. We rented audio boxes to learn about the Etruscans. We usually skipped the contraptions because they had the downside of TMI, too much information. And using them was tedious. We'd found that if we listened separately to a voice describing each numbered bit, we couldn't talk to each other, which annoyed me but didn't seem to bother Rick.

Being Etruscan neophytes, we clamped the headsets to our ears and slung the bulky boxes around our necks. In scratchy English, we learned about Etruscan vases and bronzes. Jewelry from an advanced civilization hundreds of years prior to the Roman Empire. Sophisticated pottery, gold inlaid urns, and hoop earrings from 800–300 BC. I was fascinated to see the upscale remnants of life thousands of years ago because I'd been raised on the idea that our North American Indians' heavy pottery and rough baskets were advanced. What we were seeing was at least a thousand years older.

TWO DUTCH NURSES who we'd seen in the square and at the Duomo were leaving the museum when we did. When you're far from home, a handful of random encounters is all it takes to become fast friends. The four of us shared a pizza and walked through an ongoing excavation of Etruscan tombs before heading to the bottom of St. Patrick's wells. The wells were constructed to create a secure water source for the Pope, who had retreated to Orvieto for safety in 1524. Just yesterday, by local standards.

THE MARKETS WERE closed because it was Sunday so we opted happily for a to-go supper from a restaurant. We stood at the counter and asked for *"due fette biscottate, panini"* and *"una bottiglia di vino."* We dined in our room, watching camel races in Venice on television.

SEPTEMBER 4   It was a lovely morning and we easily stashed our gear in the saddle bags, enjoying traveling lighter. First stop was to find a place to buy oil for the bike.

When that errand was completed and the tire pressure checked, we headed for a tiny hill town named Civita B. Our plan was to see it, make a U-turn, and head north, seeing hill towns we'd skipped on the way south. But we never found it and ended up in Civita C. I didn't want to give up on finding "B" so we examined the map.

"You know, we're so close to Rome, we really should go there," Rick said with his gloved finger pointing at our map.

"But you said the traffic would be so insane you didn't want to."

"I know. And it's expensive. But if we park Woody outside of the city, we could take a train or bus into the city and carry our gear in the laundry bags," he said.

"Oh lovely," I thought. The stuff dreams are made of. I'd arrive in Rome wearing dirty motorcycle boots with a laundry bag for a suitcase. My mother would be horrified. But I'd see Rome! "OK, let's go."

In another thirty minutes or so, I called out to Rick, "How close are we?" We'd been on the lookout for a likely place to park. I didn't hear an answer.

THERE'S NEVER A Park-and-Ride when you want one. The countryside turned to suburbs and suddenly we were in the middle of motor scooter mayhem, a wild swirl of motors and wheels. It was bell-jangling insanity but it had its advantages. I looked to my left at a stop light. The rider next to me was a shapely moped driver wearing blue spiky heels with a Prada bag nestled between slim legs. Ah, Rome.

IT SOUNDS UNLIKELY but Rome simply snuck up on us. Cars, trucks, and mopeds flew by like hand grenades. The drivers didn't seem angry, just noisy. And crazy. If the traffic had behaved itself in any sort of organized pattern there should have been sufficient space for nine cars across or a few dozen mopeds. But that presumes order and if there was any I couldn't discern it. I just clutched Rick's back and sat perfectly still.

WHEN THE LIGHT changed, the field of two-wheeled warriors roared off as if it was the starting line for a big race. We had no destination so my goal was to keep us upright and to not run over anyone. Such was the bedlam of Rome bustling about its business. It was too big and too expensive but plans have a way of evolving without permission. So, here we were, racing down the streets and sometimes over the sidewalks.

I LEANED FORWARD and hollered, "Stop at one of these hotels." In a few blocks, Rick swerved to the curb and I climbed off. With my helmet still on, I walked into an air-conditioned plush sanctuary. It was too expensive but I got a map and directions to something more "suitable." I'll never know what the desk man thought of a middle-aged American woman in black leathers and a helmet but I knew he'd remember me.

The next hotel was full but the concierge was either bored, intrigued, or on commission. He asked if he could make reservations for us at a different hotel. He spoke English but not in a dialect that made more than every fifth word intelligible. I hoped I'd understood the right words.

Back out in the sunshine, Rick was leaning against the bike. "Hey, I thought you took a room and forgot I was here."

I laughed. "Sorry it took so long. I think we have reservations at this hotel." I handed him a business card and climbed on.

Being lost without a destination is different from not being able to find what you're looking for. With my palms pressing the map to Rick's back, we roared off. When I thought we needed to turn, I leaned forward, hollering next left, or right, depending on what I thought we were supposed to do. We'd careen around a corner or miss it and try the next one.

We towered above the mopeds, which were short, loud, and as plentiful as mosquitos in Montana. At stoplights I waved the hotel's business card in the direction of the nearest bike, hollering "Dov-eh?" "Where?" We couldn't understand the answers but rode in the direction of pointing fingers.

In an alleyway on Del Curso we found the hotel. It was by far our most expensive but the price included breakfast and there was a flat spot to park. And we were in Rome! We emptied the saddle bags into our laundry bags and Rick gave Woody a loving pat that said, "Please be here when we come back."

Our room wasn't much larger than a closet but with its dark paneled walls, it resembled a ship's cabin. Stripping out of my clothes, I smelled like exhaust and it seemed appropriate. I was exhausted. But I was only the passenger, Rick looked frazzled.

We showered and walked through the lobby to stand on the sidewalk. "Rome," we said nearly in unison. The Eternal City.

We sat at a heavy wrought iron table on mismatching chairs. Rick ordered coffee and I, iced tea. Rick's coffee came in a cup the size of flower petals. He was travel weary, longing for big cups and free refills. I reminded him that the American kind wouldn't taste as good.

I ASKED CHRISTIE, "What do you think 'When in Rome, do as the Romans do' really means?"

She said, "It's the Golden Rule of Travel."

"Which is?"

" Adjust, adapt and accept. The triple A, of course," she said as though everyone should know that.

We'd been adjusting and adapting to local ways for three and a half months.

"Not for me," I grumbled. "Right now, I'd like a big juicy steak. New York. Medium rare. With a baked potato. And a green salad with blue cheese dressing."

"Now, don't go crazy on me. We've got three weeks of foreignness left to enjoy."

I pretended not to hear and continued. "And two sleeves of Fig Newtons." I laughed but half-heartedly.

I really did want a rare steak and Fig Newtons.

We walked away from the café and suddenly the Colosseum was in front of us. I don't know what I expected but before I could sort it out I was within touching distance of one of the greatest works of Roman engineering and the largest in the Roman Empire. Constructed in AD 80, it could seat 50,000. We joined a tour that had no fee.

Our college intern guide told tales of executions, mock sea battles, and animal hunts. Movie scenes of gladiator clashes and chariot races could have been filmed right on this spot without needing any set changes.

WE HEARD THE story of Romulus and Remus being the source of the name "Roma." The story hinged on the power of gods, changing religious attitudes, kings, and royalty. Maps of the Roman Empire showed its size from start to finish 30 BC – AD 500. The heart of Rome is history unfolding. I was learning things I should have learned in school.

SEPTEMBER 5 Breakfast in the hotel was on the second floor and over coffee we decided on our grand touring plan. The bike would stay parked. We'd walk to the Pantheon and then take it as it came.

THE PANTHEON IS a work of art and engineering even by modern standards so the fact that it was built in 150 BC is simply unbeliev-able. A 15-story building could fit under its dome. A portico of gran-ite Corinthian columns lined up in front with more behind. I stood close to one. Massive. No way small wooden boats before Christ could transport them from Egypt to Rome. But here they were.

A rectangular vestibule connected the porch to the rotunda with a central opening to the sky. It's for ventilation but doesn't allow rainfall to enter. How'd they do that? It's two thousand years old and still the world's largest unreinforced concrete dome.

A GROUP OF African tourists were wrapped in flowing brightly colored fabrics and matching head wraps. The women were vibrant. The men wore turbans and remarkable woven belts. Rick and I were in their midst, examining an obelisk that was 5,000 years old. I wondered what they were talking about, what their perspective was in comparison to mine. Without a common language, I wouldn't find out.

WE WALKED BY the balcony where the Italian crowd cheered when Mussolini declared war on America and France in 1940. Christie has a good imagination and said she could hear the clatter of Italian boots marching up the marble steps.

The building next door was the home of Napoleon and his mother. It had an enclosed balcony, designed so she could eavesdrop on street conversations without being seen. Without daytime soap operas on television, who could blame her?

AT PIAZZA NAVONA, we saw the fountain and the Basilica of St Agnes where Julius Caesar was murdered. As an English teacher, I was entranced. The stories I'd read and taught were coming to life. What a difference it would have made if my students in Los Angeles could have seen Rome. Or if I'd seen it while I was still teaching.

I looked up at the statue of a winged horse and chariot. A jet flew over. Wing on wing, the dichotomy of a jet and a winged horse. Same idea, different technology.

An archaeology dig was in process. A measuring stick marked how the street level had risen. Three feet every five hundred years. That meant that 2,000 years ago ground level Rome was twelve feet lower. Amazing.

"Even though we went underground in England to the Viking village, it's still strange to me that the ground is rising," I said to Rick.

"Me, too. American history is measured in hundreds of years. Less than three feet. It's beginning to make sense that digging up the past isn't a big career choice in our part of the world like it is here."

All roads seemed to lead to the *Foro Romano*, the Roman Forum. This was the third time we'd passed it. Again we stopped to get our bearings and to enjoy the drama. For centuries, it was the center of Roman public life: processions, elections, speeches, criminal trials, a marketplace and gladiator matches. Now it was a sprawl of building fragments and ongoing excavation.

Walking by broken pieces of columns, Rick said, "In Los Angeles these would be long gone." Before I could get him to clarify, he turned his hat backward and mimed loading chunks of Roman columns into the back of a pick-up truck. "Make a fine coffee table for my pad. Maybe I'll sell 'em to my bro's," he said, miming low-slung pants and an LA swagger. He looked like one of my high school students. While I was laughing, a small crowd formed to watch.

Rome was an easy city to walk with plenty of shady places to rest. We dined on rosemary-roasted-pork panini on the grass in front of the building where Jesus' disciples, Peter and Paul, were jailed.

I BOUGHT A pocket-size book that showed an image of each structure as it looks now, with an overlay showing it in its prime. Every time Christie pulled it out of her pack someone asked where they could buy one. We should have bought a dozen and sold them at a profit.

Taking our lives in our hands, we crossed a broad boulevard. Scooters buzzed like hornets. Buses lumbered by, belching fumes. Cars and taxis zipped through the melee. I was glad we were on foot with Woody safely, I hoped, still locked at the front of our hotel. We walked on until we found the *Bocca Della Verità*.

KNOWING A BIT of Spanish made translating other Romance languages feasible. *Bocca Della Verità*, was the "mouth of truth." Carved from marble, the man-like face is thought to be part of a first-century fountain. The most famous characteristic of the Mouth, however, is its role as a lie detector. In the Middle Ages, it was believed that if you told a lie with your hand in the mouth of the sculpture, it would be bitten off.

We stood in line and took a turn with our hands in the fountain. It wasn't a fair test of truthfulness; I told Rick I loved him. He said he loved me. Who could question the veracity of that?

HEADING FOR ANOTHER famous fountain, we walked in the direction of the Trevi. While we walked, I thought out loud. "The Romans built the aqueduct for the Trevi over 2,000 years ago and it still flows just fine."

"And it's not the only one. Rome has thirty-one other functioning fountains. In our country, I don't think water systems are built to last much more than a few decades," Christie replied.

"So you're saying that maybe the American notion that we're number one needs some re-thinking?" I laughed and Christie nodded.

LEGEND SAYS THAT a coin tossed at the Trevi ensures a return to Rome. Rick told me that tourists throw enough coins to subsidize a supermarket for Rome's needy and while I was happy to help the cause, I said, "I'll toss a coin or two but I don't really think we'll be back."

Rick agreed. "There's so much more of the world to see."

WITH A FEW coins in my right hand, I turned with my back to the fountain and flipped the coins over my left shoulder. If I wasn't ensuring a return to Rome, at least I wanted to encourage lots more travel.

Christie bought silk scarves as gifts and a $1.50 bottle of wine for the room. The label looked respectable and I reminded myself not to be in too much of a hurry to get back to the familiarity of America, where good wine wouldn't be cheap.

ALBERT, THE SHOPKEEPER who sold me the scarves, was fascinated that we were Americans traveling without hotel reservations and tour guides.

"You should write a book!" he said. "Maybe more Americans will travel like Europeans." At the time, I laughed it off, never expecting that we would do just that.

SEPTEMBER 6   It was our last day in Rome and we hadn't been to the Vatican yet. While we hadn't even planned to be in Rome, we couldn't leave without seeing the Sistine Chapel.

We didn't even consider a taxi. It would be expensive and we'd miss whatever was between us and where we were going. We had no interest in figuring out the bus schedule and we'd agreed that the bike would stay parked until we left the city, so we walked. In forty-five minutes, which included a few wrong turns and a five-minute airport-style security screening, we were inside the Vatican.

WE ARRIVED EARLY for the Pope's weekly "audience" and took empty seats, sixth row center. It wouldn't start for about an hour so we people-watched. The seats around us filled in and folks waved brightly colored scarves and tiny flags from their native countries. Our neighbors were from Peru and had come all the way to Rome primarily to be near the Pope. "El Papa," they said with incredible reverence.

Swiss guards wore costumes designed by Michelangelo that made them look like court jesters but I kept the "un-Catholic" thought to myself.

HORSES PRANCED AND the Pope's white electric cart entered. The faithful joined the chanting, "Il Papa, Il Papa." Thousands stood on their chairs to cheer so we did too. Pope John Paul II was a bent old man and had been the Pope longer than any predecessor since the first one in AD 60. The popemobile went by my chair and I privately thought he looked like he'd already died. His face was grey and he leaned at the angle of the Tower at Pisa.

"IL PAPA" ADDRESSED the crowd in a powerful voice but it quickly faded to mumbling. Even though he was clearly ailing, he spoke in Italian, then French, followed by English, German, and Spanish. He blessed individuals and groups and near the end, a dozen brides and grooms went forward. The brides were decked out in traditional white gowns and veils, the grooms in full penguin suits. I've no idea how devout you needed to be to have the Pope bless your marriage but it was probably a real big deal for those selected. We made for the exit to see the rest of the Vatican.

Entering the modern Vatican Museum, I realized we might have made a tactical error being on-campus on Pope-day. The hallways were a conveyor belt of humanity surging in a solid mass. In their midst, we were unwillingly shuffled from room to room.

IT WAS OVERWHELMING. Fourteen hundred rooms were filled with statues, paintings, and memorabilia from 3,000 years of events. But we weren't there to see them all, just the

Sistine Chapel, which I'd thought was in St. Peter's cathedral. Wrong again.

When we found the famous chapel, a loudspeaker bellowed for silence and ordered us to keep moving. It was about as charming as Dachau, although I did get a quick look at the painted ceiling. Hot, tired, and disappointed, we made our way out of the building, around the Vatican wall and into St. Peter's Basilica. The late Renaissance church has the largest interior of any Christian church in the world.

The devout waited to enter the prayer chapels and longer lines formed in front of confessionals. While the faithful lined up, we sinners walked on by. Somewhere in the vast space a choir sang. Unfamiliar languages were spoken in hushed tones and pilgrims flowed around us.

STATUES OF PRIOR popes looked down from every alcove. The sheer scale was magnificent and restored my crowd-weary spirit. Works by Michelangelo were everywhere but the one I was headed for was the *Pietà*. This famous work depicts the body of Jesus on the lap of Mary after the Crucifixion. Once there, I stood my ground and looked at the *Pietà* until I'd had my fill, partly to make up for having been shoved through the Sistine Chapel.

BACK OUTSIDE IN the glare of the sunlight, it took a few minutes to get our bearings. "Well, that was quite a day," I said, fumbling in my bag for sunglasses.

"How 'bout we find a chair," Rick said and abruptly turned left into a tiny café I hadn't even noticed. Over a small glass of wine and a biscuit, I joked that it was an appropriate communion snack but we toasted Catholicism reverently and added the memory to life's photo album.

For the last few days, Rick had been saying he needed a haircut and a few blocks later he spied a barber shop where

he got what we dubbed "The Roman Haircut." It might be called "the whole enchilada" in a different culture. Whatever the label, it's a level of service based on a cheerful attitude and the assumptive close.

A TALL, IMMACULATELY groomed barber greeted me and I brushed my hand over my crew cut, meaning that I wanted the same thing but shorter. There was a price list on the wall. A haircut was $6.

He pointed to a chair and whipped a crisp white drape into the air, snapping it like a rodeo cowboy with a lasso. When he'd artfully fastened the cloth around my neck, he stepped back and a shorter barber wielding scissors appeared.

Instead of cutting my hair, the pair began to volley the names of American movie actors back and forth. Waving a comb in the air, the tall one said, "Marlon Brando" and I nodded "yes," which meant I'd heard of him, not that I knew him. Scissors called out, "Al Pacino." Not sure what they expected, I said, "John Wayne" and they led me to a shampoo bowl. I started to object but I kind of knew at this point that I was about to get the Gucci of Italian haircuts.

While names were tossed around, my barber team marched straight down the menu, giving me every service listed. When there was no more powdering, shining, trimming, or spritzing to be done the bill was $20. I ran my hand over the top of my head, nodding enthusiastically, I exclaimed, "*E fantastico.*"

Christie was laughing and shooed us all out to the street where she took my picture with the two Italian bandits.

MUCH LATER THAT evening, I sat across a candlelit table from my handsomely turned out husband, fingering the gold necklace I'd worn since Prague. We dined on a shared platter of antipasto, aromatic truffle fettuccini, and a bottle of red wine, followed by sex under the mirrored ceiling in our hotel room.

SEPTEMBER 7 Drivers sat at stop lights like penned bulls. At one point, we were going 90 kph in a 40-zone just to keep from being trampled. Lessons I learned: Watch your mirrors. Don't pay attention to the posted speed limits. Lane lines are irrelevant. Anything goes.

SCOOTERS OOZED LIKE glue between belching cars and trucks. We rode with them. A matronly woman with a tiny cap of a silver helmet and flowing red skirts careened in front of us. A briefcase brigade of office workers in white shirts with multi-colored ties flying over their shoulders rode like Hollywood stuntmen. Diesel fumes from trucks roared by and I was at eye level with their wheels. We'd been on the road for quite a while and the madness hadn't diminished. Finally,

I leaned forward, hollering into Rick's helmet. "Honey, do you know how to get out of Rome?"

It was a few moments before he replied. With a slight twist of his head, he called out, "No, but I figure if all roads lead to Rome, one must lead out. I'm looking for it."

I leaned back, pulled my face mask back down, and relaxed. Rick was happy and we were still alive. Those were things to be grateful for.

IT WAS MORE than an hour before I found the autostrada and headed north.

"Happiness isn't ready made. It comes from actions."

– THE DALAI LAMA

CHAPTER 17

FRIENDS, FLAYOSC AND FAVORITES

PERUGIA WAS MUCH larger than I'd anticipated so we looked around a bit but rode on to find something more tranquil.

WITH ITS DARK grey limestone buildings, narrow streets, and Gothic architecture, Gubbio was a pleasure. We explored the Roman theatre, built in the first century. Augustinian friars outnumbered tourists. In their brown robes, with ropes tied around their ample waists, they looked like pairs of salt and pepper shakers waddling down the walkways. Church bells pealed and we decided to stay.

We found the Grotto Hotel and ate dinner next door. An antipasto platter for two was pâté, prosciutto, toast, eggplant, and melon with wine refills for $5.

TWILIGHT DARKENED THE streets. Cross-bows and swords were in shop windows and we learned that a traditional contest has been held without interruption since the 15th century. Local crossbow-men, in period costumes, compete with their Tuscan counterparts from Sansepolcro each May and September.

GUBBIO WAS HEAVEN until rain came down in a torrent. It turned to hail that bounced like popcorn and skittered on the cobblestones. Thunder growled and a light show flashed psychedelic shades of yellow on the dark sky.

WE DASHED BACK to the hotel, played cards, and wrote in our journals while the storm messed up the lives of the poor folks in campgrounds.

SEPTEMBER 8 I stowed the gear and checked the tire pressure while Christie went to find a phone. She called her mother and had a nice chat. Jean wasn't the least bit happy that I'd taken her daughter on this harebrained and dangerous trip. Her real beef, though, was twofold. (1) Motorcycle camping as a way to see Europe didn't carry country club panache and (2) I'd quit work. I'm not sure the objections were in that order but Christie was happy to have spoken with her and to hear in her voice a bit less displeasure.

Through both email and phone calls, she also confirmed that Cristina's in Florence was expecting us, that our Italian friend, Grazia, would meet us there, and she got directions for the home visit in southern France after that. With plans in place, we rode to Florence.

SEPTEMBER 9 It was a perfect almost-fall day. Brilliant blue sky, crisp breeze, and warm sun. We walked to Chappelle Medicee, the tomb of the Medici family. Some of Michelangelo's most famous works adorn the tombs of Lorenzo the Magnificent and his son.

We met Grazia in front of the Santa Maria Novella. She'd been a good high school friend of our oldest daughter when she was as an exchange student. She'd been like a third daughter and it was great to see her.

AFTER LOTS OF hugs, we compared family notes, shared news, and learned that she was just weeks from finishing her PhD in Archaeology. Grazia grew up on the island of Sardinia and had once lived in Florence so she was a very capable, and fun, tour guide.

First she took us to Europe's oldest pharmacy at 500 years old. Then to a fancy lunch. Grazia laughed when we told her our escapades with pricing but she just shrugged and said, "That's Italy." I felt better knowing it wasn't just for visitors.

GRAZIA STEERED US to Santa Croce, a church that houses the graves of Michelangelo, Machiavelli, and Galileo; quite the trio. We sat in a park and chatted, then crossed the Ponte Vecchio en route to the train station. We hugged goodbye and promised to email. It had been a wonderful afternoon but she was catching the 5:30 train to Genoa and then the ferry to Sardinia. She'd come a long way to see us.

SEPTEMBER 10   Woody was heavily loaded for the first time since August 30. We rode in warm sunshine, through tunnels and over viaducts into France. It was another $30 toll road day but the views of the blue Med were worth it.

In Antibes, we set up camp on rock-hard ground in time for a good stroll along the beach. Some of the gals were tanning more than their shoulders and once again I enjoyed the view.

SEPTEMBER 11   A riot of brilliant blue and yellows linens were piled on tables in Flayosc. I lusted for a tablecloth but since I didn't own a table, I resisted. Sylvette's arrival spared me. We hugged, hopped on the bike and followed her car.

Seated in the sunshine by Sylvette's parents sparkling pool, olive groves stretched to the horizon. I felt like a character in a movie instead of a woman camping her way across Europe. Sylvette caught us up on news of her husband, Don, and their lives in Panama. Her parents were quick to keep our glasses full and I sipped happily between bites from platters of bread, cheese and olives. I learned that there's nothing better than really fresh olive oil.

SEPTEMBER 12 Nursing a mild hangover, we said goodbye. In the last 48 hours we'd spoken more English, other than to each other, than since the trip began.

We roared past beach towns littered with high-rise condos lining the Mediterranean. Marinas overflowed with expensive yachts. Crowds filled the beaches. Billboards gave us a clue as to how resorty or tacky the next town might be but none looked enticing enough to make me want to stop.

A 300-MILE DAY was our outside limit and peering over Rick's shoulder I could see we'd just about reached it. We were bypassing the towns along the Mediterranean. The Med! Usually Rick was happy to stop but I agreed that this renowned stretch of real estate didn't look appealing. An interesting looking abbey was coming up at exit #38 and I hollered forward but we roared on by. Exit #40 offered an okay side road that I suggested because I was approaching melt-down.

I WASN'T INTERESTED in stopping until we passed Argelès, which looked like a seaport vacationers' town but without the condo-craze of the last hundred-plus miles. We continued a few more miles into Collioure and I was in luck. It was a charming village with a fort, beaches, and restaurants galore but the hotels were full so we rode on to Port-Vendres.

In the quaint seaside town with a colorful marina and two ocean-going freighters tied to the commercial piers, we found a hotel with just one room available. It was cheap and the room was on the top floor. We were willing to climb the stairs; after all, we didn't have much luggage. I'd been close to being in trouble for riding too long but when Christie stepped onto one of our three tiny balconies overlooking the marina her grin told me I'd been spared.

STREET CHATTER AND the smells of roasting meats and vegetables floated up from the street. After an almost-too-long day on the bike, the voices were music and the aroma a joy. We moved in and went back to the bike to collect our camp stove and galley supplies because our three tiny patios (one just off the bathroom!) were too good to leave. The hotel was admittedly tacky, but our wrought iron railings and shuttered doors overlooking the marina of working boats charmed me.

It was neither Spanish nor French they were speaking but Catalan, which I hadn't even heard of before. We were in France with a splash of Spain, two hours to Avignon, France, or Barcelona, Spain. I felt like I'd discovered it myself. A Mediterranean paradise.

SEPTEMBER 13   We started the day with coffee on our patio above the docks. Church bells. Birds. Boats. And then we went exploring, south to the Spanish border at Portbou.

In every village, painters sat at easels. And it made sense. The place was alive with color. The bright blue Med. Sailboats. Pastel buildings. Narrow streets. Flowers, pottery, vineyards, a castle, a church.

Traffic from an open air market crowded the street. While it lacked the wicker basket charm of Provence, it was lively. The air had a kelpy-sun-on-rocks smell. Fruit crates overflowed with lemons, apricots, and flies. Vendors called out.

Plastic laundry baskets were filled with brooms and threatened to topple over on a mountain of frying pans and dusty pirated CDs. Barrels of green and purple olives rolled around in dusty oil, competing for photo-ops with bundles of what Christie said was lavender and probably thyme, which she liked better than the rows of buckets filled with wriggling sterling silver. "Eels," we were told.

Favorite towns were Banyuls-sur-Mer and Collioure. We even looked in the windows of a handful of real estate offices.

AFTER OUR RIDE, Rick headed off to do the laundry, so I was alone. Sitting on one of the balconies, it occurred to me that this was the longest we'd been apart since he'd played golf in Scotland.

The evening was warm and I pulled together my own version of paella using fish that I bought right out of the nets below our balcony. We watched the town's twinkly lights and the moon over the Med. The sky was thrown open, unleashing stars to sail over the water.

We raised our glasses in a toast, "To adventure," Rick said.

"To flexibility." I replied. "And teamwork."

"Take the adventure, heed the call ... then some day, some day long hence, jog home here if you will, when the cup has been drained and the play has been played, and sit down by your quiet river with a store of goodly memories for company."

– KENNETH GRAHAME,
THE WIND IN THE WILLOWS

CHAPTER 18

SLOW AND REFLECTIVE

SEPTEMBER 14 We weren't in a hurry to leave. Sipping hot coffee on the patio, we took our time munching the flaky croissants filled with gooey fresh figs and eating the peaches we'd bought from a roadside stand the day before.

SOMETIMES, AS THE end of a good story approaches, we slow down, staving off the inevitable in order to savor the moment. And so it was with this journey. In the early weeks we'd scurried from England to Ireland, eager to see new sights. Scotland, Belgium, Denmark, Germany, Switzerland, Italy, France. Country followed country like elephants in a parade.

I had scarcely considered that our odyssey would end. Sometimes, when we were rain-soaked, cranky or travel weary, we'd almost wished it would. But now it really was nearing the end and that changed everything.

WE RELUCTANTLY SADDLED up and headed west. The ride grew more twisting and beautiful with each mile. Smooth roads and lots of turns made the miles fly by. Adding to the joy was that every

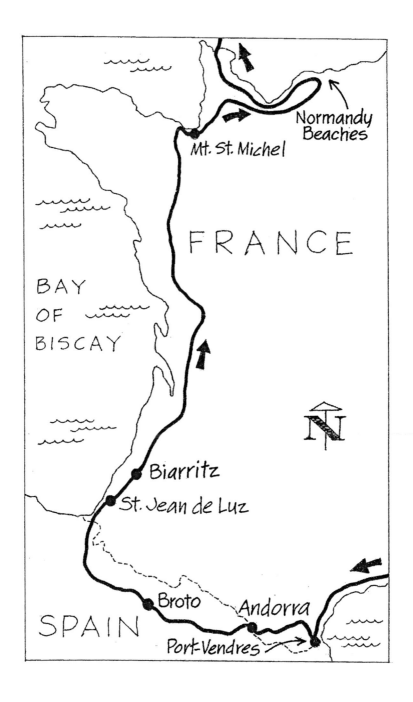

30 minutes or so we came to another medieval walled village that wasn't even on our map.

THE FACT THAT we were riding toward the Pyrenees was a surprise in itself. Back in Arizona, we'd thought we'd head northwest out of Italy, cutting across central France. But here we were, executing another unplanned twist in the route, which we'd found was the most magical path anyway.

At Eus, we walked around the grounds of a Villa France convent. At Olette we stopped for a baguette, cheese and sausage picnic. Rick flourished the knife he'd bought in Arles, making quick work of slicing the cheese and meat.

It was just the two of us, the motorcycle and miles of scenery to be inhaled. And so I breathed deeply, face to the wind, savoring the scent of the apricot trees. At the proverbial fork in the road, we had a choice between a tunnel and a mountain pass and Rick chose the 8,000-foot pass because that's what you do on a motorcycle.

AT PAS DE La Casa, traffic crawled. The congestion was reminiscent of leaving Los Angeles at rush hour and I wondered why. Then I noticed that all the license plates were French and saw the reason for the line-up. We were at the border of France and Andorra. Gas here was half the French price.

ANDORRA IS A tax-free country, tucked at the foot of 60-plus mountain peaks that soar to 10,000 feet. Compared to the medieval cities we'd grown accustomed to, Andorra was new. And so small you could hold it in your arms, which I wanted to do. We booked a room in a high-rise hotel and the price included meals. Hot springs bubbled in a 21st-century building that was a water park with dancing waters and a spa. Three hours cost $16 each, a delicious splurge.

DINNER WOULDN'T BE until 8:30 p.m. so we went shopping. Christie bought a pair of lined leather pants, just $65 including having them shortened. Booze, Havana cigars, couture clothing brands, and Swiss watches were so cheap I wished for a minivan. We did buy a fine bottle of wine for $2.

SEPTEMBER 15   Our last American-style breakfast had been a long time ago. The buffet of scrambled eggs, ham, muffins, and orange juice was a welcome surprise.

It was a short ride to the border of Spain, past fields of tobacco being dried in huts. A customs agent quizzed us at length. He held a machine gun so I tried to be patient but he must have been unaccustomed to tourists leaving Andorra and claiming so little. He insisted I'd bought cases of liquor. I just kept shrugging and pointing at our small storage spaces until he waved us through.

OVER THE SPINE of the Pyrenees, from Andorra toward the Atlantic, we rode. A village set in the ruby rocks was appropriately named Rubio. Beyond that, the road rose and fell, up rough red hills and back down to the valley floor. On the low roads, we followed a meandering stream that matched the road turn for turn. Long cool tunnels offered relief from the heat. Villages clung to the tops of each peak. Sometimes they were walled, but all were old and set amongst rocks that tilted precariously.

At Perbes we got off. Ancient crumbling walls contrasted with a riot of color in the gardens but that was the only evidence that it was inhabited. The next village perched like a cherry on a sundae crowning the hilltop. Swooping back down, we rode through narrow canyons where the blue sky disappeared in the small space between the walls.

LUNCH WAS A prix fixe dinner menu. Even though Spanish is the one language we could understand, the menu was unfamiliar. The four-course meal began with a bean, meat, and hard-boiled egg soup and kept getting better with each plate.

We rode in heavenly seclusion with no oncoming traffic or anyone apparently going our way, either. Waterfalls cascaded so close to the road that we caught the spray. I could hear Christie giggling.

At a pullout, we chatted with the rare other traveler, Brits on their way to Valencia. The woman said, "Go to Broto, you'll love it." And we did.

We chose the hotel with a large television room so we could watch the Olympic opening ceremonies. While I locked the bike in an enclosed garage, Christie walked up the road and came back with a few pieces of fruit, some interesting-looking cheeses, and a bottle of wine. We spent the rest of the evening reclined on leather sofas, snacking and watching the Olympics in Spanish.

SEPTEMBER 16   Breakfast at our little hotel was $5 for both of us. I wrote in my journal, *"Toasted baguette and honeyed croissants with cappuccino. It's day 3 of week 16 and I'm not tired of the bike, the trip, or my husband. What a miracle. We hadn't planned to ride the Pyrenees but here we are and I'm in love with them, too."*

A red-tailed hawk flew overhead with a wiggly catch in its claws. Field mice scurried over the hot rocks beside the road. Honey-colored fields stretched in a vast emptiness until Rick pointed to the right. A beret-clad shepherd was tending hundreds of sheep. Once we spotted the first one they were around every turn. We'd entered Basque country.

WE SLOWED FOR a military roadblock but they waved us on. The military presence grew as we headed west. The Basque Separatist movement had been escalating their terrorist activities and we'd seen on CNN in Andorra that the French had arrested a Basque leader.

RIDING INTO FRANCE along the coast road, we saw camp grounds lined up like airport parking lots, all empty because summer was nearly over.

We rented a cabin at Cote Basque across the road from the ocean. For $20 a night, we had a stove, refrigerator, bed linens, a porch, and five chairs. Heaven on earth. In Saint-Jean-de-Luz, we bought food for two days.

SEPTEMBER 17 It was a lazy morning with breakfast on our deck. I pulled out a sleeve of stickers we'd chosen in Antibes, Banyuls-sur-Mer, and Andorra. Deciding where to put them, I peeled away the wrinkled corner of one I'd messed up using the back of my Langloise knife.

We rode into St.-Jean-de-Luz. The Saint-Jean-Baptiste church is where Louis XIV married Maria-Theresa in 1660. His first cousin, as well as the Spanish Infanta, she became the Queen of France. The little town is also the birthplace of Ravel, the composer famous for the Bolero, which premiered in 1928 but became wildly popular after being featured in the soundtrack of the 1980 movie 10. The town was very proud if the signage was to be believed.

THE HOUSES WERE half-timbered in Stratford-on-Avon style but decked out in red and white instead of Elizabethan brown. Restaurants offered trays and literally boats full of food to passersby. Open boats had been filled with ice and mounded two feet high with fish, olives, cheeses, apricots and plums. There was so much food I had the feeling we were walking on a giant placemat.

We'd forgotten most of our high school French and we spoke no Basque, so we had no way of knowing if this was a special occasion, a holiday, or a regular event, but we knew we loved it. Men in berets marched out of the church and women in brightly colored skirts walked with them. We followed the parade into Plaza Louis XIV.

MEN WEARING THREE-CORNERED hats trimmed in white fur joined the parade. The townspeople danced. We did, too. We didn't see a single American or a place to sit but we filled plates with shellfish and sat on a bench near the quay but close enough to hear the music.

SEPTEMBER 18   While Rick washed Woody, I wrote in my journal. *"A feeling of serenity has overtaken me and I realize it has to do with not having a single wish in the world. I don't want to be anywhere else or with anyone else. I don't need something to eat or drink. I'm not looking forward or back. I'm entirely comfortable in the present. This is the trip I wanted to take and it's even okay that it's nearing its end."*

IT WAS A total kickback day of lying in the sun, doing laundry and bike chores. We walked along the bluff overlooking the Atlantic. The horseshoe bay was dotted with windsurfers and sailboats. The beach was busy with splashing toddlers, topless women, and elderly folks dressed like they'd just left church. Christie said she'd seen some tan Frenchmen in skinnier than jock-strap swimsuits, but I must have been looking elsewhere.

We chatted with our British neighbors, who seemed quite staid until we saw them on the beach. Camilla dropped her top and changed into a bikini bottom right next to us. When I stopped staring, I turned to say something to Christie and she was topless, too! I do love France.

SEPTEMBER 19 We rode the coast road north to explore. Biarritz is an elegant old lady of a sea town with a wide beachfront walkway and graceful church facing the sea and the plaza. We put on our best "we only look like we can't afford it" smiles and asked for a tour of the grande dame of hotels, picturing my parents vacationing there.

THE RITZY COASTAL resort was *très élégant* and the hotels were huge and expensive. Whenever a town catered to Americans, I knew I'd find a *USA Today* and I did. I also bought a USA sticker. It was the first time we'd seen one and, after all, it was the country where the ride began.

Back at camp, we had a visit from a Frenchman we'd met the day before. He was Loic Peron and he carried a jug of sweet wine and a Basque cake. Loic wanted to run a business idea past us, the only Americans he'd ever met. Christie produced a not-surprising classy spread of brie, baguette, and grapes to accompany his cake and wine.

While we feasted, he explained his idea of importing 1950s American furniture to the French countryside. He thought it would sell easily and at a profit. I'm not sure why simply being Americans would qualify us as import/export gurus but we did our best to be honest without discouraging him.

LOIC TOLD US that the coast area where we were camped was protected from development by conservationists, which explained the open spaces we hadn't seen elsewhere. We told him that we'd been riding across Europe for almost four months and had seen Brits in France, Germans and Dutch, everywhere but very few Frenchmen except in France. He shared that French workers typically get seven weeks' paid vacation and that they use the time to take long vacations but almost always within France because they didn't typically speak a second language.

SEPTEMBER 20   We packed up slowly and reluctantly left the cabin. Riding through Saint-Jean-de-Luz in the early morning light, a scarf of dust twirled behind. A shopkeeper parked her bicycle; another turned a key in a lock. "Closed" signs were turned over to begin a new day. I waved a wistful goodbye and hollered at no one but my psyche, "I'll be back!"

RODE NORTH THROUGH Bayonne, a charming old town, to the seaside village of Arcachon. We rode all day just covering miles. At Saint-Malo, a castle sat right on the waterfront, boats tugged on their moorings. Stops like that were a good stretch of the legs but we kept going.

At Mont-Saint-Michel, we booked two nights in a room just a mile from the much photographed Benedictine Abbey that juts into the English Channel on a clump of rocks. We explored the village inside the Abbey but kept one eye on the tides. It would be an island about 10:00 p.m. and our room was on the other side.

SEPTEMBER 21   It was Rick's 57th birthday. And Woody's birthday, too, since we'd bought the cycle on this day, one year ago. And our last full day on the European continent. Party themes and menus occurred to me but there was no time to celebrate.

It was "D" day for us. Sword. Juno. Gold. Omaha. Utah. We'd do them east to west. I was only nine months old when the world's power tilted on these sites but the names of the invasion beaches were very familiar.

The Germans had fortified the mouth of the River Seulles, so on 6 June 1944, at 7:45 a.m., amphibious tanks were launched at Courseulles-sur-Mer. Most of them sank because of the ocean swell. Those that succeeded in reaching the beach opened fire on the Germans, enabling the 7th Brigade to advance inland and to liberate Courseulles-sur-Mer in a few hours.

In a small museum at Arromanches we learned about that town's contribution. The Germans had occupied France for four years when the Brits built a breakwater and dragged it across the water to this port. Using old sunken ships as ballast, they created a landing pier for artillery and supplies. It was this engineering accomplishment that helped the Allies destroy the German Air Force. It was the beginning of the end of the war.

Port-en-Bessin is a seaside town. Waves galloped to the beach like horses, their manes whipped to a frenzy by the wind. Grey clouds scudded past, allowing slats of afternoon sunshine to spill out. The smell of seaweed combined with fishy smells from sidewalk restaurants but we weren't there for lunch. Our mission was 1944. On June 7 the British launched the attack and forty men were killed. On the morning of June 8, the British freed Port-en-Bessin.

We parked in Vierville-sur-Mer, on the right bank of the Douve River estuary. I got emotional walking on the beach, trying to envision the landing. Bravery must have mixed with terror in the young men, boys really.

At Pointe de Hoc we stood in the craters caused by the artillery. So much carnage. By August much of Europe had been won back.

It was an emotional day. "Morally, how could the Swiss stay neutral when all this was going on so close by?" I asked Rick.

"It's hard to understand now, isn't it," he said quietly.

EVERY SEASIDE TOWN had war memorials and monuments marking where the allied forces had landed. The remains of German gun emplacements and bunkers were haunting reminders. Inland, too, there were monuments at nearly every bend in the road. It seemed there wasn't a square yard that hadn't been a battlefield.

We rode on to Vierville-sur-Mer and there it was again. A commemorative square in the center of town. "6 June 1944: The U.S. Army 29th Division 116th Infantry, and 2nd and 5th Rangers Battalions landed on Dog Green sector of Omaha Beach."

Standing in a German bunker on the cliff above the beach, I wondered, "How?" How could these young men scale the cliff and face their enemy? The young Germans faced nearly certain death, too, trying to hold their ground. I respected the crosses of the dead soldiers on both sides.

The cemeteries reminded me of the Ryan family back at the Rock of Cashel in Ireland. Brothers dying within days or weeks of each other. We walked through the American cemetery, a sea of 9,000 simple white crosses aligned in neat rows.

TAKING A DEEP breath and trying to clear our heads, we were climbing back on the bike when a man waved at us to wait. He scurried over as fast as his cane and limp allowed. "You are Americans. I need to thank you." His enunciation was impeccable but I had no idea what he was thanking us for. His hands fluttered like moths around his bobbing beret. We waited for him to catch his breath. "Your mothers sent their boys to a place they didn't know. Across an ocean." He batted at tears and went on. "To save us. To free us. Bless them all." There wasn't time to discuss it. He scuttled away.

Heading back, we rode past miles of French farmhouses. Wisteria climbed over the boxy grey and yellow stone buildings. They looked unchanged from whatever century they were built in. For an hour, we rode past fields of grain, more cattle, hedges, and farmhouses. But the images of war and D-Day were engrained.

Rick came to a complete stop when a French woman slowly, very slowly, escorted her two dozen cows across the road. In her left hand she held a tattered red flag. It fluttered like some kind of crosswalk signal. We sat not ten feet from her. She had cheeks like shriveled apples; her muddy mid-calf boots exposed mud-splattered legs. Her skirt was mud flecked, too. Otherwise, the pale green fabric dotted with yellow flowers could have been her church outfit. Oh my.

"If you live each day as if it was your last, some-day you'll most certainly be right."

– GARY FRIEDMAN,
FORMER CEO, RESTORATION HARDWARE

CHAPTER 19

THE END

SEPTEMBER 22   We rode away from Mont-Saint-Michel through swirls of fog until the sun broke free and light cascaded over the countryside.

On the ferry to England, we met a fellow cycle rider. He shared our picnic and invited us to follow him and stay at his house in Dorset. We showed our passports and rode onto British soil. It was a beautiful Friday afternoon and sailboats dotted the busy harbor.

ALAN WAS A retired motorcycle policeman and rode a white K100S. Keeping up was the hardest thing I've ever done. Flying past heavy traffic on the highway, rode the shoulder. It wasn't much wider than our loaded bike. I could feel the tension in my shoulders and my eyes were riveted on his license plate. Every few miles he turned in the saddle to check our progress. You would have thought he was swiveling on a bar stool instead of on a speeding motorcycle. I thought I'd gotten pretty good after 113 days and he said he'd ride slowly but I was no match. Later, he told me that very few applicants qualify for police motorcycle duty in England. I believed him.

HE PULLED OFF at a thatched roof inn and we followed. Over coffee with his pals, I had a sudden longing to rent a cottage. To stay. To see if I could become a local, too. A week from today we'd be back in America. If I was going to start life over, why not here?

Alan's wife wasn't at home so I stirred together some pork and vegetables, chopped apples into sauce, and arranged biscuits and tea on the platter I'd bought in the Josefov neighborhood of Prague. The three of us listened to the BBC on the radio and the guys smoked cigars in the living room.

SEPTEMBER 23 We woke to a bonny blue morning in Dorset. Christie put out coffee and toast and we set off to explore the coastal villages of Beer, Branscombe, and Sidmouth. Christie offered to write the town names as we rode so we could find our way back. She said it'd be like Hansel and Gretel leaving a trail of bread crumbs. At first I thought it was a bit silly but after a couple of hours I agreed that following a trail of village names was the only way to retrace our steps.

WE RODE THROUGH Shute, Colyton, and Kilmington and walked a coast path. The roads were bridle path–wide but open to two-way traffic. Fifteen-foot hedgerows towered on both sides. The roads serpentined in a pattern like a sailor's knot, circling back on themselves with lots of curves and nary a straight-away. I thought it was charming but I knew Rick had to pay close attention.

Stopped for crab sandwiches and a proper pot of tea. At Sidmouth we climbed the tower stairs to a popular, if the parking lot was any indication, garden stop on a rocky promontory above the crashing surf.

It was a balmy 75 degrees and felt like summer. Grand, old-style hotels lined the boardwalk and Brits were out in force enjoying the sunshine. Some strolled the gardens and others rested in striped sling chairs. All were dressed in what looked like 1940s attire.

SEPTEMBER 24 We were headed to see Paul and Carol in Surrey, whom we'd met at the harp music car-park in Ireland. We said goodbye to Alan and left for London in light rain. It wasn't light for long. I stopped to take my glasses off because they were completely fogged. Waterproof gear has a limit and ours was previously met. My pants leaked. Christie's jacket absorbed instead of repelling. Our shoes squished.

THE THUD OF British raindrops was as thick as porridge. Rain fell in biblical proportions and we looked for a place to get warm because dry wasn't possible.

When we stopped, my hope was for a bowl of thick soup and dry socks. I got my first wish. Wrapping my hands around a mug of potato-corn chowder so thick my spoon stood up straight, I was thrilled that we could have refills.

I felt badly leaving puddles in Paul and Carol's pretty hallway but after a change of clothes, with our wet gear hung to dry on rods in their bath, everything looked brighter.

AFTER DINNER AT a neighborhood pub, Paul and I went out to his shop and ended up swapping tank bags. He showed me the work he was doing on an antique Land Rover.

SEPTEMBER 25 We'd planned to leave but Paul had good relations with his neighborhood motorcycle shop so we arranged for BMW service instead and decided to tour London while Carol and Paul were at work.

WE RODE THE bike to the shop in town and caught the train from Guilford to Waterloo station in London. Classic taxis in black and burgundy, red double-decker buses, bobbies in tall hats, and the prissiness of business men wearing skinny ties and small collars. London. It would have seemed trite if I hadn't seen it with my own eyes.

At St. Paul's Cathedral, we stood in front of the crypt of Florence Nightingale and silent prayer was called for on the hour. We climbed to the top of the dome. The views were sweeping but reconfirmed my impression that this wasn't an easy city to tour with long distances between sights.

LONDON IS EUROPE'S biggest city, with over seven million residents, and we were too travel-weary to tackle it. We bought a two-day bus pass, which seemed like a good idea because it was nearly the same price as the one day.

First was the Tower of London. The historic castle on the north bank of the River Thames has been an armory, a treasury, menagerie, the home of the Royal Mint and the current home of the Crown Jewels. Before we went to see them, a witty Beefeater led us through the executioner's block that dispensed with troublesome heirs to the throne and a couple of Henry VIII's wives. It was a great tour for guys in the group but the gals tugged the pace along, eager to see the Jewels.

COMMONLY CALLED "REGALIA," the crowns are the ones the monarchy wears when they attend formal ceremonies. The Imperial State Crown is encrusted with nearly 3,000 diamonds, 300 pearls, a dozen emeralds, a bunch of sapphires, and five rubies. It looked too heavy to wear but since they wouldn't let me try it on, I couldn't find out. We filed by 25,000 other jeweled items and after a while all that wealth got repetitive.

ON DRURY LANE, we read the playbills at the Theatre Royal, vowing to return on a future trip for a proper theatre night. The Royal opened in 1663, making it the oldest continuously used theatre in London.

At Covent Gardens, we bought flowers for our hosts. The market stalls opened in the 1600s. Soon we'd leave all this antiquity, replacing it with American strip mall efficiency.

We took the subway to Waterloo and from there, the train back to Guilford. Christie chatted with a businessman in a brown suit, seated across from her. When he stood to get off, he patted my shoulder and said, "In all the years I been ridin' the train, I never afore had such a conversation." I smiled and nodded but I wasn't surprised.

We arrived in a major rainstorm thirty minutes after the motorcycle dealership should have closed. In a hurry, we hopped in a taxi. It was our first taxi of the whole trip. The bike was ready, the bill reasonable and they'd stayed open past closing for us. What service.

CAROL'S BOUQUET TOOK a beating in the downpour. We rode through dark unfamiliar streets, without rain gear, and got irrevocably lost. When Rick finally agreed that we needed help, I asked for directions and we managed to untangle the web of streets and found March Cottage.

More wine, excellent olive and anchovy pasta, and conversation till past midnight was my favorite part of the day.

SEPTEMBER 26 Amidst hugs and hollering "see you somewhere," we rode down Paul and Carol's driveway, toward the inn near Gatwick airport. In Horsley, we got off where we'd begun on June first. They still had our duffle bags.

We dumped our gear and took the train back into London to use the other half of our two-day bus pass.

The changing of the guard at Buckingham Palace happens just twice before noon so we went there first. We arrived just in time and stood against a black iron railing. The mounted guards rode past us, up "The Mall" and returned. I got a big kick out of the tall bearskin hats.

Trafalgar Square, as a center for protest, was a place I wanted to see. There weren't any protesters on our visit but about 35,000 pigeons and their obvious mess made me want to protest. Poop was everywhere.

But Christie was humming happily, "Feed the birds, tuppence a bag, tuppence, tuppence, tuppence a bag," she crooned from the musical *Mary Poppins*. She can't carry a tune but I recognized it anyway. And yes, there they were. The bird ladies sat on benches, feeding the feral, pooping, messy birds.

We popped into a pub for some local color and a last chance at pub grub. Christie had said in Amsterdam that maybe our best look at a country was what was happening today. With that in mind, I led us to a dark-paneled-smoky-private-club-leather-wingback booth. Sipping a warm shot of Scotch and munching meat pasties and pickled eggs definitely felt British.

Back on our tour bus, we rode past Big Ben, the most prominent visual symbol of London. Since the mid-1800s it's been noted for reliability, chiming on cue throughout the bombings of the '40s.

I REALLY WANTED to see "Speaker's Corner" in Hyde Park, so we used the hop-off privilege. When I was on my high school's speech team, my fellow orators and debaters thought it would be fun to erect such a spot, taking turns persuading our classmates on some random subject. We were going to call ours, "Screamer's Corner." Today the man with the megaphone sounded like an American congressman, shouting for passers-by to hear his point of view. Kind of humorous, but it's not called "Speaker's Corner" for nothing.

Carts peddling soft swirl vanilla and chocolate ice cream with a chocolate cookie swizzle stick sticking out like a straw were "very London" to my way of thinking, so I indulged. They'd never get to the finals in a taste test with Italian gelato but at least I'd learned that firsthand.

Licking my dripping cone, we rounded a corner to find a clutch of American tourists with similar cones. The woman closest to me was wearing unseasonably skimpy clothes. Too short shorts and a sleeveless top on a body that shouldn't have considered such an outfit in the last four decades. A monstrous bus parked nearby, its belching motor idling. Mercifully, the name tag–wearing Americans found their way back to the bus without further scandalizing the neighborhood.

We walked past the Prime Minister's residence at 10 Downing Street and on to Westminster Abbey. A queue stretched around the corner. I left Rick in line and skirted its right edge until I got to the front. *Closed at 4:30 p.m. for services* the sign read. I looked at my watch. It was 4:45. I walked 100 yards back to where Rick stood and motioned for him to follow. Slipping past the line again, I poked my head in the dark opening where three women swathed in black stood in the shadows.

In a whispered reverent tone, I asked, "May we enter? We're here for Evensong."

"Oh, yes, come in, my dears," came the sweet reply accompanied by three jowly jaws wreathed in smiles.

Once again, we had detoured off the tourist path. I felt a bit smug and just a bit guilty bypassing the long line. I had read in my Rick Steves guidebook that the Abbey closed to tourists during services but that worshipers were always welcome, and I'd used the information to my advantage, as he intended.

Inside, choir voices engulfed us. It sounded like angels lived in the vaulted stone ceilings. The 700-year-old structure has hosted and laid to rest, kings, queens, statesmen and soldiers, poets, priests, heroes and villains.

I LIKE SYMMETRY, so it was fitting to end a journey that began with a prayer in the chapel in Arizona at Evensong in Westminster Abbey.

Back outside, London was growing dark. We walked through Soho and Chinatown to Victoria Station and the train ride "home."

SEPTEMBER 27   At a leisurely pace, we rode Woody to the airport cargo office. I recognized the man who'd been less than helpful 119 days earlier. He seemed the same. I didn't think I was.

We caught a bus back to the inn and walked to the laundromat. Tomorrow we'd fly home. Back to the land of the familiar. I'd longed for it on occasion but now, I wasn't so certain.

SEPTEMBER 28   We had time for a full breakfast before the shuttle would take us to the airport. I watched the owner of the inn across the room. She slowly sipped tea from a small yellow and white cup. Carefully setting it down, she methodically spread butter on her toast before tapping the end off her egg with the same knife. She set the knife next to a jar of marmalade and looked up. Our eyes met. She held my gaze over spectacles that slid further down her nose while she plunged her spoon into the yolk of her soft-boiled egg. I vowed to remember the pace. To memorize it.

Just three hours later, roaring down the runway, the plane gathered speed and the wheels retracted with a loud clunk. London tilted away. Suspended at 40,000 feet, Rick and I sat a few inches apart, as we had for most of seventeen weeks.

TRIPS, LIKE STORIES, come to an end. The moment arrives when we close the book, sigh, and contemplate the characters. We're satisfied if the author took us on a journey of words through a pleasurable adventure and successfully tied up the loose ends. And if the author turned a few memorable phrases we're extra pleased. Yet we're saddened that it's over. And so it was for us.

IN THE COMING years we would settle into new jobs and buy a house. But "home" was never again a street address. Home was wherever we were.

If you never did, you should. These things are fun and fun is good.

– THEODORE SEUSS GEISEL (DR. SEUSS)

APPENDIX A

Best planning tools: We couldn't locate any helpful camping or motorcycle guides. All-around best travel info was the **Rick Steves series.**

<u>Surprises:</u>

Rick: We went to Rome
Christie: We didn't go to Paris or Venice
Rick: Christie didn't need fancy shoes, skirts or scarves
Christie: We stayed married

<u>Times we wished we were someplace else:</u>

Rick: 5
Christie: 3
# of times I wrote *"Life is Good"* in my journal: 11
# of times I dumped the bike: 4 (and that's the whole truth)

APPENDIX B

<u>18 Countries</u>: England, Wales, Ireland, Northern Ireland, Scotland, Belgium, Netherlands, Germany, Denmark, Sweden, Czech Republic, Austria, Italy, Switzerland, Monaco, France, Andorra, Spain.

<u>Favorite Towns:</u>

Ireland: Kenmare, Allihies
Scotland: Dornoch, St. Andrews
Netherlands: Edam, Hoorn
Denmark: Ribe
Czech Republic: Cesky Krumlov
Austria: Hallstatt
Italy: Manarola in the Cinque Terre
Northern Spain: Broto
France: Saint-Jean-de-Luz

Best/Worst:

BEST PICNIC SITES	Northern Ireland
MOST CAMPING AVAILABLE	France, Scotland
CHEAPEST CAMPING	France
MOST EXPENSIVE CAMPING	Austria, Switzerland
MOST B + Bs	Republic of Ireland
BEST MOUNTAIN PASS RIDE	Sustenpass in Switzerland
LEAST FAVORITE AFTERNOON	Füssen castles
FAVORITE AFTERNOON	spa at Baden Baden
BEST CAMP BATHROOM	Saint-Jean-de-Luz, France
WORST CAMP BATHROOM	Brugge, Belgium
COLDEST	Scotland
HOTTEST	Cinque Terre
MOST PERSISTENT RAIN	July
MOST PERSISTENT SUN	September
BEST BREAKFASTS	England, Ireland, Scotland
MOST EXPENSIVE	Sweden
LEAST EXPENSIVE	Czech Republic
FUEL MOST EXPENSIVE	Scotland/England
FUEL LEAST EXPENSIVE	Andorra

We awarded "Five stars" to the following:

Irish pubs
Ribe, Denmark, night watchman tour
Amsterdam spirit and canals
Edam coffee
Austrian greeting "Gruss Gott"
Czech prices, architecture

APPENDIX C

PACKING LIST

Tank bag:

Main compartment: Maps, guide books, language guides, hats (2), chamois, windshield cleaner, tire gauge.

3 side pockets: (1) camera, lock cable. (2) sun lotion, bug spray, aspirin. (3) rags, playing cards, journals, photos/map from home and "business" cards with our name and email addresses.

Rear (trunk):

Tent, stove and fuel, 1 pot, chamois towels, 2 bowls, laundry line and soap. Coffee, picnic food, dishtowel, 2 cloth napkins, silverware (1 sharp knife, 2 forks and spoons), spice bag, 1 spatula, can opener, wine opener and stopper, dish soap, clothespins and tent light.

Waterproof bag on top trunk:

Cycle cover, metal plate for kickstand, light rain jackets, warm gloves, rain pants, 1 backpack, sleeping bags, pillows. Bungee on top: coffee mugs, skillet.

2 side Jesse bags:

Personal wardrobe rolled with rubber bands and inside ziplock bags. Includes: U.S. stamps, envelopes, passport photocopies, checkbook, key to the pick-up truck in storage. Bathroom kit with medicines, shampoo, lotion.

Waterproof bags strapped on each: bed mats, poles to make them chairs. Tent poles.

Shoulder purse: Extra cycle key, wallet, glasses, lip balm, 2 passports.

Purchases:

Necklace, charm, plate, knife, boots, skillet, gloves, tent, jacket, knickers and knee highs, aftershave, leather pants, radio, Christmas ornaments.

Gifts: 2 leather bags, leather book cover, 2 scarves, 1 apron, golf towel.

Total: $1,215.

APPENDIX D

Places slept	# nights
England	13
Wales	2
Ireland	12
Scotland	8
On ferry	1
Netherlands	4
Belgium	2
Denmark	3
Sweden	0
Germany	13
Czech Rep	5
Austria	7
Switzerland	11
Italy	21
Spain	1
Andorra	1
France	15

Stayed in 60 places
Set up/put away tent 20 times

Locations slept	# nights
B&B, hotel	52
Tent	44
Camping cabin	17
Ferry, friend, other	6

CPSIA information can be obtained at www.ICGtesting.com
Printed in the USA
BVOW012350270513

321640BV00001B/1/P

9 781592 998593